Present Yourself 2
Viewpoints

Steven Gershon

CAMBRIDGE
UNIVERSITY PRESS

CAMBRIDGE UNIVERSITY PRESS

Cambridge, New York, Melbourne, Madrid, Cape Town, Singapore, São Paulo, Delhi

Cambridge University Press
32 Avenue of the Americas, New York, NY 10013-2473, USA

www.cambridge.org
Information on this title: www.cambridge.org/9780521713306

First published 2008

Printed in Hong Kong, China, by Golden Cup Printing Company Limited

A catalog record for this publication is available from the British Library

Library of Congress Cataloging-in-Publication Data
Gershon, Steven.
 Present yourself 2: viewpoints / Steven Gershon.
   p. cm.
 Summary: "Present Yourself is a presentation skills course for adult and young adult learners of English,
 developed within the framework of a general conversation course" – Provided by publisher.
 ISBN 978-0-521-71330-6
 1. English language – Textbooks for foreign speakers. I. Title. II. Title: Present yourself two.

 PE1128.G393 2008
 428.0076 – dc22

                          2008027118

 ISBN 978-0-521-71330-6 student's book and audio CD
 ISBN 978-0-521-71331-3 teacher's manual

Art direction, book design, photo research, and layout services: Adventure House, NYC
Audio production: Richard LePage and Associates

Contents

Plan of the book

Getting ready pages 2–7	**Preparing to present** Doing a survey to get to know classmates Learning about the steps for a presentation	**Introducing a classmate** Completing a brainstorming map Learning about the organization of a presentation Listening to a classmate introduction

Unit	**Topic** focus	**Language** focus	**Organization** focus
1 **A motto for life** pages 8–19	Discussing people's mottoes Talking about personal values	Explaining the meaning of a motto Relating a motto to a past experience	All units include focusing on brainstorming ideas and creating an outline for a presentation.
2 **Young people today** pages 20–31	Talking about survey topics, questions, and results Surveying classmates	Describing a survey Reporting survey results	
3 **Dream vacation** pages 32–43	Discussing types of vacations Planning the perfect vacation	Talking about vacation destinations Talking about activities and accommodations	
4 **How the world works** pages 44–55	Taking a trivia quiz Talking about process topics	Introducing a process presentation Explaining a process	
5 **In my opinion** pages 56–67	Discussing issues Completing an opinions survey	Relating an issue and expressing an opposing opinion Supporting opinions	
6 **In the news** pages 68–79	Talking about news headlines Words to describe news stories	Introducing news stories Talking about details in news stories	

Presentation tips	My classmate introduction
An introduction to what good presenters do	Preparing and giving a classmate introduction

Presentation focus	Presentation skills focus	Present yourself!
All units include focusing on the introduction, body, and conclusion of a presentation, and listening to a model presentation.	Making and using presentation notes Tip: Making eye contact when speaking	Brainstorming ideas Creating an outline Giving a presentation about a personal motto
	Explaining visual aids Tip: Using visual aids effectively	Brainstorming questions and doing a survey Creating an outline Giving a presentation about the survey results
	Asking lead-in questions Tip: Timing and intonation of lead-in questions	Brainstorming ideas Creating an outline Giving a presentation about a dream vacation
	Inviting audience questions Tip: Answering audience questions	Researching a process Creating an outline Giving a presentation about the process
	Emphasizing an opposing opinion Tip: Using body language to emphasize an opinion	Brainstorming ideas Creating an outline Giving a presentation about an important issue
	Leading a group discussion Tip: Encouraging audience participation	Researching a news story Creating an outline Giving a presentation about the news story

To the teacher

In our rapidly globalizing world, effective communication skills are becoming more and more important for success – academically, professionally, socially, and personally. The way we interact within a group can affect the quality and success of our relationships. Just as important, the effectiveness with which we communicate in front of a group can have a great impact on our achievements in the world – opening many doors of opportunity and rewarding possibility. The *Present Yourself* series focuses on developing students' communication skills so that they have the confidence to take advantage of the many opportunities in their lives to present their ideas, experiences, knowledge, and opinions in front of a group.

Present Yourself offers a process approach that emphasizes the interdependent step-by-step decisions and tasks that are involved in planning, writing, and delivering an effective presentation to an audience. These steps include selecting a suitable topic; considering the language needed to talk about the topic; brainstorming ideas for the content of the presentation; organizing the ideas into an introduction, body, and conclusion; employing specific physical and verbal skills to enhance the delivery of the presentation; and, finally, completing a self-evaluation once the presentation has been given. Throughout this step-by-step process, the main goal is to provide students with a readily transferable set of skills they can use to give effective presentations on a range of topics in a variety of situations.

Present Yourself 2, Viewpoints focuses on topics that encourage students to speak about points of view beyond their personal experiences. The book includes six main units and one introductory unit. The introductory unit acquaints students with the process of planning a presentation and offers an entry point to giving a presentation by having students introduce a classmate. Each of the six main units guides students through the entire presentation process with engaging speaking activities, focused listening tasks that provide relevant topic input, and clear functional language support that targets both vocabulary and useful sentence patterns. Moreover, the core of each unit provides a complete model presentation that students use to help them construct their own presentations based on that unit's topic.

The topics of the six main units are loosely graded in level of difficulty, ranging from presenting survey results in unit two, to explaining a process in unit four, to talking about a news story in unit six. However, as we all know, every class is different, so please feel free to pick and choose units according to your students' interests, class level, and available time.

I hope you and your students enjoy *Present Yourself*. I have enjoyed writing it and wish you success with presentations in your classroom.

Regards,

Steve Gershon

How a unit works

Each unit contains six lessons to guide students through the process of building an effective and engaging presentation. Each lesson, with the exception of the first lesson, builds on the previous one in order to provide students with the necessary skills to create and deliver their own presentations.

Topic focus

This lesson helps students to think about the topic and what they already know about it. The activities introduce useful topic-based vocabulary and encourage students to interact with each other through surveys, questionnaires, quizzes, and interviews. When students finish this lesson, they will have generated ideas that they can use later in the unit when they begin to plan their own presentations.

Language focus

This lesson encourages students to notice useful target expressions and sentence patterns they can use to talk about the unit topic. Students also listen to different speakers use the target language in the context of giving a presentation, and perform task-based listening activities. Students consolidate the target language through a semicontrolled speaking activity at the end of the lesson.

Organization focus

This lesson teaches students how to select ideas from a brainstorming map and organize them into a presentation outline that includes an introduction, a body, and a conclusion. Students are asked to notice which ideas from a brainstorming map have been included as main topics in an outline and to complete the outline with additional notes. Finally, students have an opportunity to listen to the complete presentation as they check the completed outline.

Presentation focus

In this lesson students focus on a model presentation written from the outline in the **Organization focus**. Students focus on the introduction, body, and conclusion of the presentation to see what information is included in each section. While looking at a cloze version of the model presentation, students predict the items to complete each section. They then listen to the complete presentation and check their answers.

Presentation skills focus

At this stage of the unit, students are ready to focus on a specific linguistic or physical skill related to the actual delivery of their presentation. In each unit the presentation skill is first presented visually. The order of the following activities varies depending on the presentation skill, but in every unit students read a section of a presentation to observe the presentation skill in action. They also have an opportunity to practice the presentation skill with a partner, or in a group, in a controlled speaking activity.

Present yourself!

In the last lesson of the unit, students plan, organize, and give their own presentations based on the unit topic. First, students brainstorm ideas for their topic and create an outline for their presentation. Then they practice on their own before giving their presentations to the whole class or in a group. A self-evaluation form for each unit is included at the back of the book for students to evaluate their own presentations once they're finished.

Author's acknowledgments

I would like to thank the following reviewers for their valuable insights and suggestions:

Yasmine Bia, **ELS Language Centers**, Vancouver, British Columbia, Canada; Madonna Carr, **University of Illinois at Chicago**, Chicago, Illinois, U.S.A.; Frank Claypool, **Osaka College of Foreign Languages**, Osaka, Japan; Karen Cronin; Alison Doughtie, **Mohawk Valley Community College**, Utica, New York, U.S.A.; Kirvin Andrew Dyer, **Yan-Ping High School**, Taipei, Taiwan; Karen Englander, **Universidad Autónoma de Baja California**, Baja California, Mexico; Lisa Feasby, **Korea University**, Seoul, South Korea; Denise Fenwick, **Kobe Women's University**, Kobe, Japan; Duane Gerussi, **Kansai Gaidai University**, Osaka, Japan; Linda Gogliotti, **Aichi University**, Aichi, Japan; Oscar Gutiérrez Pulido; Angela Harris, **Tennessee Foreign Language Institute**, Nashville, Tennessee, U.S.A.; Ray Hartman, **Sungkyunkwan University**, Seoul, South Korea; Midori Iba, **Konan University**, Kobe, Japan; Kanae Koike; Yayoi Kosugi, **Keio University**, **Tokyo Eiwa Women's University**, Tokyo, Japan; Masashi Kubono; Susan Lafond, **Guilderland High School**, Guilderland, New York, U.S.A.; Huei-Chih Christine Liu, **Shu-Te University**, Kaohsiung County, Taiwan; David McMurray, **The International University of Kagoshima**, Kagoshima, Japan; Kazuhiro Nomura, **Kobe City University of Foreign Studies**, Kobe, Japan; Geraldine Norris, **University of Shizuoka**, Shizuoka, Japan; Mark Senior, **Konan University**, Kobe, Japan; and Rena Yoshida, **J.F. Oberlin University**, Tokyo, Japan.

A special thanks to the **editorial** and **production** team at Cambridge University Press who worked on this course:

Sue Aldcorn, Karen Brock, Sarah Cole, Brigit Dermott, Deborah Goldblatt, Vivian Gomez, Louisa Hellegers, Alejandro Martinez, Julia Meuse, Kathy Niemczyk, Sandra Pike, Christie Polchowski, Kate Powers, Tami Savir, Jaimie Scanlon, Satoko Shimoyama, Rachel Sinden, Lori Solbakken, and Shelagh Speers.

Thanks to the Cambridge University Press **staff** and **advisors**:

Harry Ahn, Yumiko Akeba, Kenneth Clinton, Heather Gray, Tomomi Katsuki, Jennifer Kim, Robert Kim, Kareen Kjelstrup, John Letcher, Hugo Loyola, Andy Martin, Carine Mitchell, Catherine Shih, Howard Siegelman, Ivan Sorrentino, Herman Su, Irene Yang, and Ellen Zlotnick.

I would like to express my sincere thanks to Richard Walker for his participation in this project as a contributing writer. As well, I would like to thank all of my "Techniques in Speech" students at J.F. Oberlin University, from whom I continue to learn how to teach presentation skills. Finally, my thanks to Britt and Becky, who never fail to offer useful suggestions whenever I ask them to "have a look at this activity and tell me what you think."

To the student

Dear students:

What is your greatest fear? Seeing a big spider? Walking alone on a dark street? Having a serious illness? Being in an earthquake? These are some of the answers that people often give in popular magazine surveys. Surprisingly, the one fear that seems to be on everyone's top-ten list is public speaking. That's right. Most people say that giving a presentation to a group of people is more frightening than seeing a spider, having an illness, or being in an earthquake!

People's fear of public speaking is understandable for a few reasons. First, when we give a presentation, we feel that we are being judged. And nobody wants to sound foolish or be boring – especially in front of a lot of people. Moreover, giving a good presentation involves a variety of communication skills that are very complex – even for native speakers. And of course it is even more difficult (and frightening!) when you are speaking a foreign language, with so much new vocabulary and grammar to remember.

For learners of English, giving a good presentation involves more than using English correctly. It involves choosing a suitable topic for your audience and deciding what you want to say. It also involves organizing your ideas into an attention-getting introduction (beginning), a clear body (middle), and a memorable conclusion (end). And, finally, it involves using your voice, gestures, posture, and eye contact to connect with the audience. All of these skills seem like a lot to learn, but with study and practice anyone can master the skills to be a great presenter!

So, why is it useful to learn presentation skills? It's simply because most of us will have to give a presentation or speech at some time in our life – whether we want to or not. It may be for school, work, a conference, or for a social occasion, such as a wedding, party, or club event. The purpose may be to share something personal about someone or yourself, to inform an audience about a specific topic, to explain how to make or do something, or to persuade people to change their opinion on a topic. Whatever the purpose, any time we speak to a group of people about a topic, we are giving a presentation. This means that presentation skills are very useful life skills.

Present Yourself 2, Viewpoints will help you to develop the communication skills you need to speak clearly, effectively, and confidently in front of any group – small or large. I hope you have fun using ***Present Yourself***, and I am sure your classmates will enjoy the presentations you give.

Good luck!

Steve Gershon

Getting ready

Preparing to present

1 Classmate interviews

A Think about your new classmates. What would you like to know about them?

B Read the interview topics and add one more. Then write a question for each topic.

Interview topic	Question	Classmate	Answer
Family	How many brothers and sisters do you have?	Mia	three brothers, two sisters
Hometown			
Free-time activities			
A favorite food			
A favorite song or movie			
A recent vacation			
_____			

C Complete the chart in Exercise B. Ask a different classmate each question.

D Tell the class about some of your classmates.

"Mia has a big family. She has three brothers and . . . "

2 Presentation steps

A Dan always follows these steps when he gives a presentation. Number the steps in order from 1 to 5.

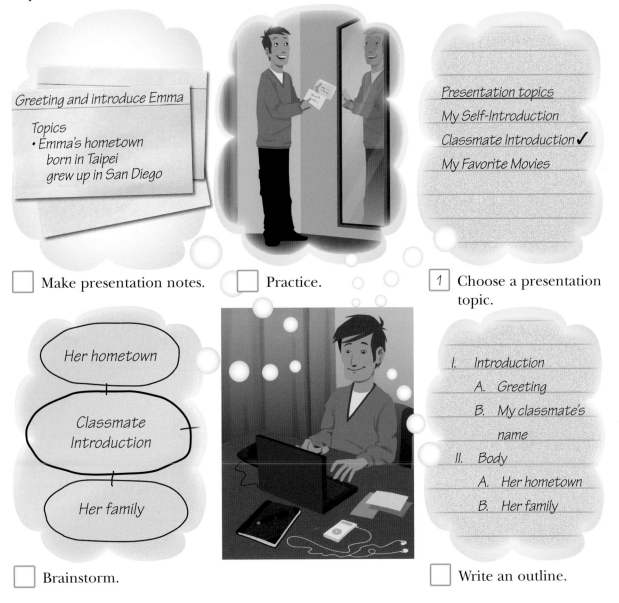

☐ Make presentation notes. ☐ Practice. 1 Choose a presentation topic.

☐ Brainstorm. ☐ Write an outline.

B 🔘 2 Match the steps in Exercise A to Dan's advice. Then listen and check your answers.

Dan's advice

_____ Write down as many topics and details as you can think of.

_____ Use note cards and write only brief phrases.

_____ Go over your presentation notes out loud, and time your presentation.

__1__ Think about your audience. Select something that will interest them.

_____ Organize the main topics and details.

Introducing a classmate

1 Brainstorming

A Dan planned a presentation to introduce a classmate. Read his notes.
Then check (✓) the five topics he included in his brainstorming map below.

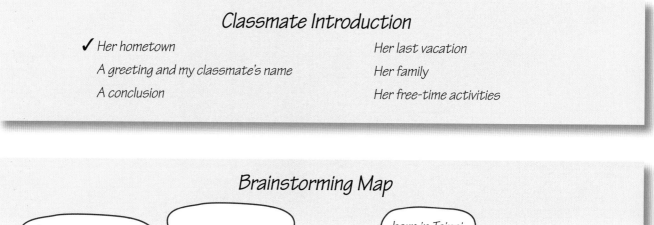

Classmate Introduction

✓ Her hometown

A greeting and my classmate's name

A conclusion

Her last vacation

Her family

Her free-time activities

Brainstorming Map

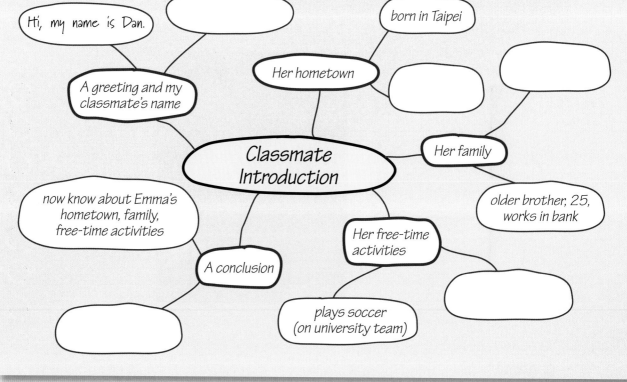

Hi, my name is Dan.

born in Taipei

Her hometown

A greeting and my classmate's name

Classmate Introduction

Her family

now know about Emma's hometown, family, free-time activities

older brother, 25, works in bank

A conclusion

Her free-time activities

plays soccer (on university team)

B Read Dan's additional notes for his presentation. Then use his notes
to complete the brainstorming map in Exercise A.

- Thank you for listening.
- small family, parents in Taipei
- grew up in San Diego

- introduce Emma
- plays guitar
✓ • Hi, my name is Dan.

2 Organizing

A Notice the information Dan included in his presentation.

▶ A greeting and his classmate's name

Hi, my name is . . . / I'm . . .   *I'd like to introduce . . .*

▶ The topics he plans to talk about

I'm going to tell you about . . .

   ▶ Topic 1: his classmate's hometown

   She's from . . .   *She was born in . . .*   *She grew up in . . .*

   ▶ Topic 2: his classmate's family

   She has a small / big family.   *Her parents live . . .*

   She has a(n) older / younger brother.

   ▶ Topic 3: his classmate's free-time activities

   When Emma has free time, she . . .   *In her free time, she likes to . . .*

▶ A conclusion

Now you know a little about Emma, her . . .   *Thank you for listening.*

B ◉ 3   Guess the missing words in Dan's presentation. Then listen and check your guesses.

Classmate Introduction

Hi, my _____name_____ is Dan. Today I'd like to

_____ our classmate Emma. I'm

_____ to _____ you about her

hometown, family, and _____ activities. Emma

_____ born in Taipei. However, she _____

_____ in San Diego, California. She has a

small family. Her parents live in Taipei, and she _____ an

older _____ who lives in California, too. He's 25 and

works in a bank. When Emma has _____ time, she

plays soccer. She's even on the university team! She also plays the

guitar. Now you _____ a little about Emma, her

hometown, family, and free-time activities. _____

_____ for listening.

Presentation tips

A Complete the sentences below with words and phrases from the box.

Make brief notes	Think about	Use simple visual aids
✓ Make eye contact	Relax	Speak loudly and clearly
Use gestures	Practice	Smile and say "Thank you"

TIPS FOR PRESENTERS

1 <u>Make eye contact</u> with the audience as you speak. ☐D

2 _____ , take a deep breath, and wait until the audience is quiet. ☐

3 _____ to show meaning. Make them slowly and clearly. ☐

4 Don't say, "Finished." or "That's all." _____ . ☐

5 _____ many times. ☐

6 _____ that everyone can see. ☐

7 _____ how you can do better next time. ☐

8 _____ , and use your voice for stress and emphasis. ☐

9 Don't memorize your presentation. _____ to guide you. ☐

B What do good presenters do before, during, and after their presentations? Write *B* (before), *D* (during), or *A* (after) after each tip in Exercise A.

C Choose two tips you think will be important for your first presentation. Tell a partner.

"I think two important tips are 'Make eye contact with the audience as you speak,' and 'Don't memorize your presentation.' How about you?"

My classmate introduction

Interview a classmate. Then prepare and give a one- to two-minute presentation to introduce your classmate.

A Interview a classmate. Use the interview topics and questions from page 2. Then complete the brainstorming map with topics and information you want to include in your presentation.

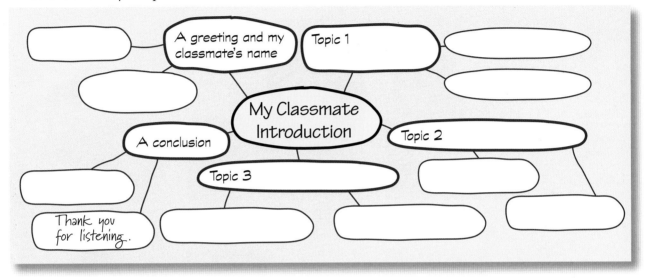

B Use your brainstorming map to complete these notes for your presentation.

My Classmate Introduction

A greeting and my classmate's name _____
The topics I plan to talk about Today I'm going to tell you about _____
_____ .

Topic 1 _____ Details _____
_____

Topic 2 _____ Details _____
_____

Topic 3 _____ Details _____
_____

A conclusion Now you know a little about _____
_____ .

C Make final notes for your presentation on note cards. When you finish, practice the presentation silently a few times. Then practice out loud with a partner.

D Work in groups. Take turns giving your presentations.

A motto for life

Topic focus

1 This is me.

A Read these people's personal mottoes. What do you think they mean? Tell a partner.

"I think 'Laughter is the best medicine' means . . . "

Laughter is the best medicine.

1 Kenji, Japan

If at first you don't succeed, try, try again.

2 Kathy, United States

Make every day count.

3 Michel, France

The best things in life are free.

4 Rosa, Brazil

Shared joy is double joy.

5 Abdul, Canada

Look before you leap.

6 Mei-li, China

B Match the people's mottoes in Exercise A to the sentences below. Then compare answers with a partner. (There is one extra sentence.)

____ Experiencing things with others enriches your life.

____ You should try to enjoy each day of your life.

____ A good education is the key to a successful life.

____ Simple things in life make us happy, not material things.

_1_ A sense of humor can make you feel better.

____ You should consider a situation carefully before acting.

____ Don't give up too easily.

C Which sentence in Exercise B do you agree with the most? Why? Tell the class.

"I agree that doing things with others makes life more fun because . . . "

2 My personal values

A What are your personal values? Why? Tell a partner. Use personal values from the box, or your own.

> **Personal values**
>
> being kind to others   enjoying your work   getting an education   taking risks
> ✓ enjoying life   following dreams   keeping good relationships   valuing money

"Getting an education is one of my personal values because . . . "

B Which personal values shape these mottoes? Match the personal values in Exercise A to the mottoes below. Then compare answers with your partner.

Mottoes	Personal values
Life is not a rehearsal.	*enjoying life*
Never stop learning.	_____
Always do what you are afraid to do.	_____
Money makes the world go around.	_____
A smile can brighten someone's darkest day.	_____
Make new friends but keep the old. One is silver, and the other is gold.	_____
Aim for the impossible, and you'll achieve the improbable.	_____
Choose a job you love, and you'll never have to work a day in your life.	_____

C Choose your favorite motto from page 8 or the list above. Write the motto and the personal value that shapes it on a separate piece of paper.

D Ask two classmates about their mottoes. Complete the chart. Then share the information with the class.

"What's your motto?"   *"Which personal value shaped your motto?"*

Classmate	Motto	Personal value
Tom	Always do what you are afraid to do.	taking risks
1.		
2.		

"Taking risks is one of Tom's personal values, so he chose the motto 'Always do what you are afraid to do.' He . . . "

Language focus

1 Mottoes and their meanings

A 💿 4 Listen to Josh, Yumi, and Andy talk about their personal values and mottoes. Check (✓) the personal value that has shaped each person's motto.

1. Josh	**2. Yumi**	**3. Andy**
☐ getting an education	☐ enjoying life	☐ enjoying your work
☐ enjoying life	☐ valuing money	☐ getting an education
☑ following dreams	☐ being kind to others	☐ taking risks

B 💿 4 Listen again. Complete the mottoes and circle the correct meanings.

	Motto	**Meaning**
1. Josh	_____Life_____ is what you make of it.	People have more *control* / *friends* than they think.
2. Yumi	Variety is the _____ of life.	Life is more *successful* / *interesting* if you have different experiences.
3. Andy	People who _____ make _____ don't make anything.	Mistakes are an *effective* / *important* part of learning.

C Work with a partner. Choose two mottoes you like from pages 8 and 9. Then take turns explaining their meanings.

💬 Explaining the meaning of a motto

Defining **This means that**	
Paraphrasing **In other words, That is,**	it's important to keep learning new things.

"A motto that I like is 'Never stop learning.' This means that it's important to . . . "

2 Mottoes and experiences

A 💿 5 Now listen to Josh, Yumi, and Andy talk about experiences when their mottoes helped them. Check (✓) each person's experience.

1. Josh
   - ☐ failed a history class
   - ☐ failed an entrance exam
   - ☐ failed a piano exam

2. Yumi
   - ☐ started university
   - ☐ traveled abroad
   - ☐ got a new job

3. Andy
   - ☐ was invited to a concert
   - ☐ took guitar lessons
   - ☐ was asked to join a band

B 💿 5 Listen again. What did Josh, Yumi, and Andy do? Number their actions from 1 to 3 in the order you hear them. (There is one extra action for each person.)

1. Josh
   - 2 took extra classes
   - 3 did practice exams
   - ☐ made a study schedule
   - 1 focused on weak areas

2. Yumi
   - ☐ made a list
   - ☐ did research
   - ☐ got information
   - ☐ met managers

3. Andy
   - ☐ practiced even more
   - ☐ learned from his mistakes
   - ☐ started singing
   - ☐ took extra lessons

3 My life experiences

A Think of an experience when a motto helped you. Write about it on a separate piece of paper.

Motto	What I did
Laughter is the best medicine.	• felt sad, disappointed
	• friends made me laugh, felt better
The experience	• decided to practice and study more
failed driver's license test	• took test again — passed!

B Work in groups. Take turns talking about your motto and experience. How has the motto helped you?

💬 Relating a motto to a past experience

This motto has helped me **I've relied on this motto**	a lot. several times. in many situations.	**For instance,** **For example,**	when I . . . two years ago . . .
I try to live my life by this motto	when I can. as much as possible.		

"I chose 'Laughter is the best medicine.' This motto has helped me a lot. For instance, when I failed my driver's license test . . . "

Organization focus

1 Tim's motto

A Look at the picture of Tim. What do you think his personal values are? Why?

B Read Tim's brainstorming notes for his presentation about his motto. Check (✓) the eight topics he included in his outline on page 13.

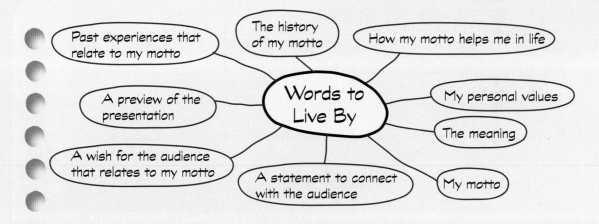

C Read Tim's additional notes for his presentation. Then use his notes to complete the outline on page 13.

- found bag in park, returned it to hotel
- how my motto helps me in life
- honesty
- reminds me I can make the world a better place
- doesn't take a lot of effort to be kind to others

2 Tim's outline

💿 6   Listen to Tim's presentation. Check the notes you added from Exercise 1C on page 12.

Words to Live By

I. Introduction
A. A statement to connect with the audience: If you're like me, you enjoy helping people and making them feel good.

B. My personal values
   1. being kind to others
   2. _____
   3. relationships with friends, family

C. A preview of the presentation
   1. my motto and its meaning
   2. past experiences that relate to my motto
   3. _____

II. Body
A. My motto: A candle loses none of its light by lighting another candle.

B. The meaning
   1. when you light one with another, the first one stays just as bright
   2. _____

C. Past experiences that relate to my motto
   1. _____
   2. lost wallet on train, someone handed it in

III. Conclusion
A. How my motto helps me in life
   1. makes me appreciate help from others
   2. helps me to be honest
   3. _____

B. A wish for the audience that relates to my motto: remember you can be a candle, too

Presentation focus

1 Introduction

Notice the information Tim included in his introduction on page 15. Guess the missing words.

> ▶ A statement to connect with the audience
>
>   *If you're like me . . .*   *I'm sure you'll agree that . . .*
>
> ▶ His personal values
>
>   *. . . is one of my personal values.*   *Some other things I value include . . .*
>
> ▶ A preview of the presentation
>
>   *Today I'm going to share . . .*   *Then I'll go on to talk about . . .*
>   *Finally, I'll tell you . . .*

2 Body

Notice the information Tim included in his body on page 15. Guess the missing words.

> ▶ His motto
>
> ▶ The meaning
>
> ▶ Past experiences that relate to his motto

3 Conclusion

Notice the information Tim included in his conclusion on page 15. Guess the missing words.

> ▶ How his motto helps him in life
>
>   *My motto helps me . . .*   *It makes me . . .*   *It also reminds me . . .*
>
> ▶ A wish for the audience that relates to his motto
>
>   *Remember that . . .*

4 Tim's presentation

🔊 6 Listen to Tim's presentation. Check your guesses.

Words to Live By

Introduction

If you're like me, you enjoy helping people and making them _____ good. Being kind to others is one of my personal values. Some other things I value include honesty, and my relationships with friends and _____ . Today I'm going to share my personal _____ and explain its meaning. Then I'll go on to talk about some past _____ that relate to my motto. Finally, I'll tell you how my motto _____ me in life.

Body

My motto is "A candle loses none of its light by lighting another candle." In _____ words, when you light one candle with another, the first candle doesn't go out; it stays just as bright. This _____ that it doesn't take a lot of effort to be kind to others, and it makes us feel good.

I try to live my life by this _____ as much as possible. For instance, a few years ago, I found a bag containing a wallet, camera, and other valuables on a park bench. There was a hotel card in the bag, so I took it straight to that hotel. In the hotel lobby, a young man, in a panic, was in the middle of telling the staff that he'd lost his _____ somewhere. He was really pleased to see his bag and was very grateful that I'd brought it to the hotel. He offered me some money as a reward, but I didn't accept it.

Recently I lost my wallet on the train, but luckily someone handed it in to the station lost-and-found office. I went to pick it up, and this time, I was the one feeling grateful. It really made my day.

Conclusion

My motto makes me _____ help from others, and it helps me to be _____ . It also reminds me that I can make the world a _____ place by doing something kind for someone else. Remember that you can be a candle, too, and it's easy to light many other candles each and every day. Thank you.

Presentation skills focus

1 Presentation notes

When you give a presentation, use clear, organized notes as a reference while you speak.

Look at the pictures and read the "dos and don'ts" of making and using note cards. Then do the note-taking exercises on page 17.

> *My motto is "If at first you don't succeed, try, try again." This means that you shouldn't give up. In other words, you should keep trying, even when you don't succeed the first time. This motto has helped me several times. For example, two years ago, I applied for a job, but I didn't get hired, because I needed work experience.*

Don't write too much on each note card.

> *• Motto: If at first you don't succeed, try, try again.*
>
> *• Meaning*
>   *follow your dreams*
>   *don't give up*

Do leave lots of space on each note card.

> *• Experience that relates to my motto*
>   *I applied for a job but didn't get hired because I needed work experience.*
>   *I did an internship at a small company.*
>   *Then I applied again for the same job and was hired!*

Don't write full sentences.

> *• Experience that relates to motto*
>   *applied for job, didn't get hired, needed work experience*
>   *did internship at small company*
>   *applied again, hired!*

Do write short phrases.

Don't memorize your presentation.

Do use your note cards to remember what you want to say.

Presentation tip

Eye contact will help you make a connection with the audience. Don't read directly from your notes. When you need to check your notes, look down and think about what you are going to say. Then look up, make eye contact with the audience, and speak.

2 Your turn

A Read the example from a presentation. Can you complete the note cards for this presentation? Use short phrases to complete the two cards.

> My motto is "Just jump." This means that you shouldn't think too much before doing something. In other words, you should take action when you have an opportunity. I've relied on this motto a lot. For instance, about a year ago, I had a chance to do a homestay in the U.K. I was nervous about being away from my family and friends for a whole year, but I decided to go. Well, it was the best experience of my life . . .

• Motto: ___Just___ ___jump___   1
• Meaning
   don't _____ too _____
   _____ _____ something
 	
   take _____ _____
   _____ have opportunity
	• Experience 2
	   a _____ ago, had _____
	   _____ _____ homestay in U.K.
	
	   nervous, but decided _____ _____
	
	   _____ experience of my _____

B Work with a partner. Cover the presentation so you can only see the note cards in Exercise A. Take turns giving the presentation from the notes.

"My motto is 'Just jump.' This means that . . . "

C Choose two mottoes you like. On a separate piece of paper, write the mottoes and their meanings in note form.

> Motto: Never stop learning.
> Meaning: important to keep learning new things

D Work with a partner. Take turns presenting your mottoes and their meanings. Practice using your notes only for reference and making eye contact as you speak.

"A motto that I like is 'Never stop learning.' This means that it's important to . . . "

Now **present yourself!**

- **Turn to page 18.**
- **Prepare your presentation.**

Present yourself!

Give a presentation about your personal motto.

1 Brainstorming

Choose a personal motto. Write it in the center of the brainstorming map. Then add as many details as you can for each brainstorming topic.

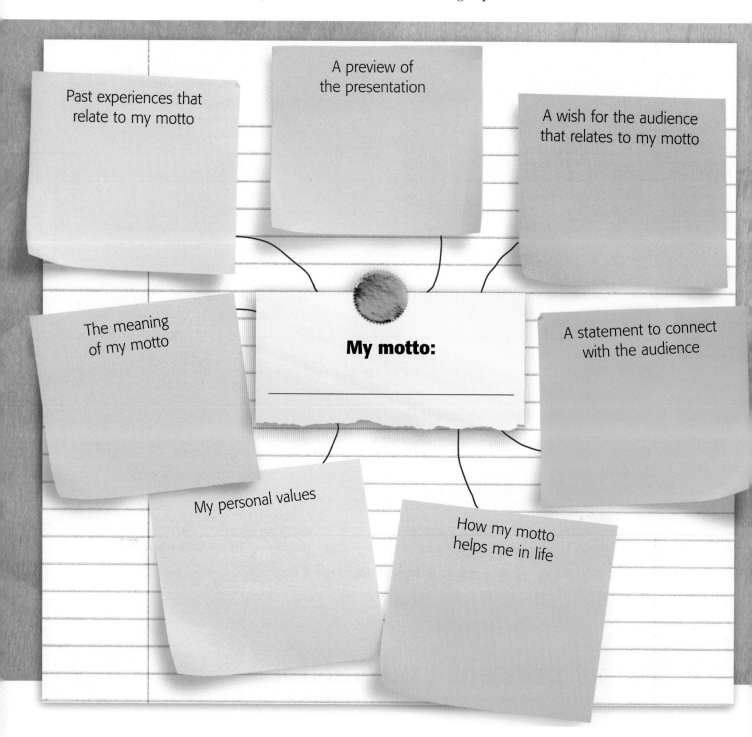

Past experiences that relate to my motto

A preview of the presentation

A wish for the audience that relates to my motto

The meaning of my motto

My motto:

A statement to connect with the audience

My personal values

How my motto helps me in life

2 Organizing

Use your brainstorming notes from Exercise 1 to complete the outline. Then
make note cards from your outline and practice your presentation.

_____
(title)

I.   Introduction

    A. A statement to connect with the audience

    _____

    B. My personal values

    _____

    C. A preview of the presentation

    _____

    _____

II. Body

    A. My motto

    _____

    B. The meaning

    _____

    C. Past experiences that relate to my motto

    _____

    _____

III. Conclusion

    A. How my motto helps me in life

    _____

    B. A wish for the audience that relates to my motto

    _____

3 Presenting

Give your presentation to the class. Remember to use
clear, organized notes as a reference while you speak.

> Don't forget to complete
> your self-evaluation on
> page 80 after your presentation.

2 Young people today

Topic focus

1 Survey questions

A Read the announcement for these presentations about young people. Which ones look the most interesting? Which survey results surprise you?

> ## LECTURE SERIES
> ## Young People Today
>
> **Come listen to these researchers share the results of their surveys.**
>
> **"Schools Today" – Special talk by Professor David Collins**
>
> ☐ Only 10 percent of young people today say they study over an hour a day.
>
> ☐ One-third of all high school students think that school is not challenging.
>
> **"Teen Spending Habits" – Presented by Dr. Kana Suzuki**
>
> ☐ Most teens say they receive over $100 a month from their parents.
>
> ☐ Forty percent of 18-year-olds say they go shopping every weekend.
>
> **"Youths' Values and Attitudes" – Find out from Dr. Tina Thomas**
>
> [a] Half of all young people believe they can make a difference in the world.
>
> ☐ Two-thirds of teens say friends are very important in their lives.

B What questions do you think the researchers asked? Match the questions to the survey results in Exercise A.

a. Do you think you can change the world?

b. How much time do you spend on homework?

c. What do you value the most in your life?

d. How often do you buy new clothes?

e. Do your parents support you financially?

f. Would you say that your schoolwork is too difficult, or not difficult enough?

C Think of three more topics that would be interesting to ask young people about. Then share them with the class.

"I'm really interested in . . . "

2 Youth survey

A Read the survey topics and questions. Then add your own survey topic and question.

Survey topics	Questions

1. Shopping habits	How often do you buy new clothes?
	    a. two or three times a week
	    b. about once a week
	    c. once or twice a month

2. Cell phone use	What do you use your cell phone for the most?
	    a. making calls
	    b. sending messages
	    c. browsing the Internet

3. Part-time jobs	What do you think is the most important feature of a part-time job?
	    a. good pay
	    b. friendly coworkers
	    c. enjoyable work

4. _____	_____ a. _____ b. _____ c. _____

B Ask three classmates the questions in Exercise A. Write their answers in the chart.

"How often do you buy new clothes? a. two or three times a week?
b. about once a week? c. once or twice a month?"
   "I'd say c. Once or twice a month."

Topic	Classmate 1	Classmate 2	Classmate 3
1. Shopping habits	once or twice a month	two or three times a week	once or twice a month
2. Cell phone use			
3. Part-time jobs			
4. _____			

C Work with a partner. Take turns talking about your survey results.

"I asked three classmates about their shopping habits. Two people said
they buy new clothes once or twice a month. One person said he buys . . . "

Language focus

1 Describing a survey

A 💿 7 Listen to Sun Hee, Ken, and Paula talk about their surveys. What are their topics? Number them from 1 to 3. (There is one extra topic.)

☐ News preferences

☐ Exercise habits

☐ TV-viewing habits

☐ Career goals

B 💿 7 Listen again. Complete the missing information about their surveys.

	Number of people	Age range	Gender
1. Sun Hee	____ teenagers	____ to ____	____ girls / ____ boys
2. Ken	____ young adults	____ to ____	____ men / ____ women
3. Paula	____ university students	____ to ____	____ males / ____ females

C Work with a partner. Imagine you are Sun Hee, Ken, or Paula. Take turns describing your survey.

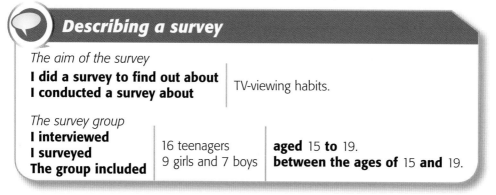

Describing a survey

The aim of the survey
I did a survey to find out about
I conducted a survey about | TV-viewing habits.

The survey group
I interviewed
I surveyed
The group included | 16 teenagers
9 girls and 7 boys | **aged** 15 **to** 19.
between the ages of 15 **and** 19.

"I did a survey to find out about TV-viewing habits. I interviewed . . . "

2 | Survey results

A 📀 8 Now listen to Sun Hee, Ken, and Paula report their survey results. Check (✓) all the number expressions you hear.

1. Sun Hee	☐ 47%	☐ 33%	☐ one-third	☐ 20%	☐ one out of five
2. Ken	☐ 28%	☐ 45%	☐ one-quarter	☐ 25%	☐ 2%
3. Paula	☐ 20%	☐ 3%	☐ one out of ten	☐ 10%	☐ two-thirds

B 📀 8 Listen again. Complete the visual aids with the correct percentages.

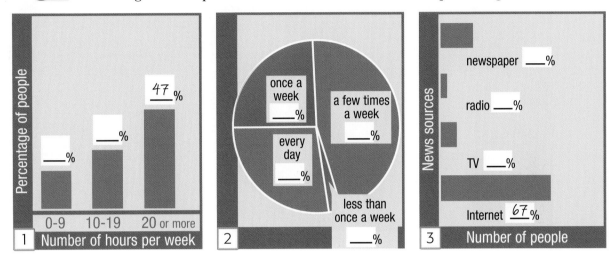

3 | My class survey

A Take a class survey. Write a topic and one survey question on a separate piece of paper. Then ask your question and write down your classmates' answers.

B Report your survey results to the class.

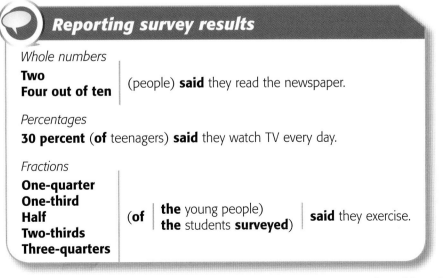

Reporting survey results

Whole numbers

Two
Four out of ten | (people) **said** they read the newspaper.

Percentages

30 percent (**of** teenagers) **said** they watch TV every day.

Fractions

One-quarter
One-third
Half | (**of** | **the** young people) | **said** they exercise.
Two-thirds | | **the** students **surveyed**) |
Three-quarters

"I did a survey to find out about transportation. Two people said . . . "

1 Hannah's youth survey

A Look at the picture of the people Hannah surveyed. What do you think the survey topic was? What do you think the results were?

B Read Hannah's brainstorming notes for her youth survey presentation. Check (✓) the eight topics she included in her outline on page 25.

Young People's Eating Habits

A summary of the results

The best fast foods

A description of the survey group

A question about healthy foods

General information about the topic

The aim of the survey

My conclusion and recommendation

A question about eating habits and how healthy they think they are

A question about junk food and fast food

C Read Hannah's additional notes for her presentation. Then use her notes to complete the outline on page 25.

- 25 percent, pretty healthy
- group included 11 women, 7 men
- young people buying more fast food than ever
- find out about university students' eating habits

- University officials should make more healthy foods available.
- one-third eat vegetables every day
- 75 percent eat fast food at least once a week

2　Hannah's outline

9　Listen to Hannah's presentation. Check the notes you added from Exercise 1C on page 24.

Young People's Eating Habits

I.　Introduction

　　A.　General information about the topic

　　　　1.　young people's eating habits worse than ever

　　　　2.　_____

　　B.　The aim of the survey: _____

II.　Body

　　A.　A description of the survey group

　　　　1.　interviewed 18 university students aged 18 to 25

　　　　2.　_____

　　B.　A question about eating habits and how healthy they think they are

　　　　1.　23 percent, very healthy

　　　　2.　_____

　　　　3.　half of the students, unhealthy eating habits

　　C.　A question about healthy foods

　　　　1.　about 50 percent eat at least one piece of fruit every day

　　　　2.　_____

　　　　3.　20 percent eat vegetables once or twice a week

　　D.　A question about junk food and fast food

　　　　1.　two-thirds eat junk food every day

　　　　2.　_____

　　　　3.　only two students never, or almost never, eat fast food

III.　Conclusion

　　A.　A summary of the results: Most students do not have healthy eating habits.

　　B.　My conclusion and recommendation

　　　　1.　Students don't have enough convenient and healthy food choices.

　　　　2.　_____

Presentation focus

1 Introduction

Notice the information Hannah included in her introduction on page 27. Guess the missing words.

> ▶ General information about the topic
>
> *Experts say that young people's . . .* *These days, young people . . .*
>
> ▶ The aim of the survey

2 Body

Notice the information Hannah included in her body on page 27. Guess the missing words.

> ▶ A description of the survey group
>
> ▶ A report of the survey results
>
> • the questions asked
> • the number of people and what they answered

3 Conclusion

Notice the information Hannah included in her conclusion on page 27. Guess the missing words.

> ▶ A summary of the results
>
> *The results of this survey show that . . .*
>
> ▶ Her conclusion and recommendation
>
> *From this survey, I can conclude that . . .* *I think university officials should . . .*

4 Hannah's presentation

 9 Listen to Hannah's presentation. Check your guesses.

Young People's Eating Habits

Introduction

Experts say that young people's eating _____ are worse than ever. These days, young people are buying more _____ food than ever, too. Well, I did a survey to _____ out about the eating habits of university students, and I think you'll find the results very interesting.

Body

For my survey, I _____ 18 university students aged 18 to 25. The group _____ 11 women and 7 men. Now I'd like to report the results of my survey. First I asked the students about their eating habits, and how healthy they think they are. Twenty-three percent said they were very healthy, and 25 percent answered they were _____ healthy. But here's the interesting part: Half of the university students said they have unhealthy eating habits. So, what are university students eating? Well, first I asked about healthy foods. As this chart shows, about 50 percent of the students said they eat at least one piece of fruit every day. But only _____ , or 33 percent of them, said they eat vegetables every day. Twenty percent of the students _____ said they eat vegetables only once or twice a week! And what about unhealthy foods? Well, I asked about junk food and fast food, and as this graph illustrates, around two-thirds of the students surveyed said they eat junk food every day. As this table explains, 75 percent of the students surveyed said they eat fast food at least _____ a week! Only two students said they never, or almost never, eat fast food. The reason most students gave for eating fast food was that they are very busy, and fast food is quicker and more convenient for them than healthy food.

Conclusion

The results of this survey show that most university students do not have healthy _____ habits. From this survey, I can conclude that university _____ don't have enough convenient and healthy food choices. They need more. I think university _____ should make more healthy foods available to students on campus. Thank you.

Presentation skills focus

  Explaining visual aids

Use simple visual aids to help your audience understand your survey results.

A Look at the visual aids. What information is being explained?

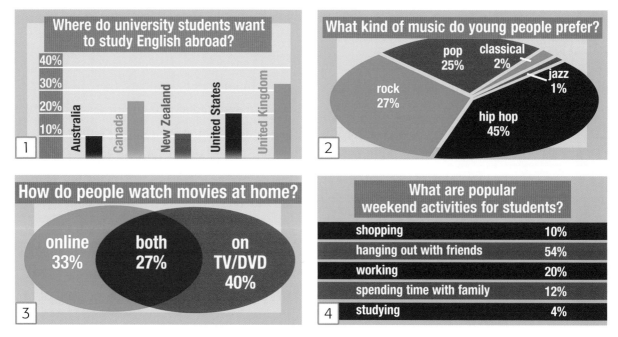

Where do university students want to study English abroad?

1 — bar graph: Australia, Canada, New Zealand, United States, United Kingdom (40%, 30%, 20%, 10%)

What kind of music do young people prefer?

2 — pie chart: pop 25%, classical 2%, jazz 1%, rock 27%, hip hop 45%

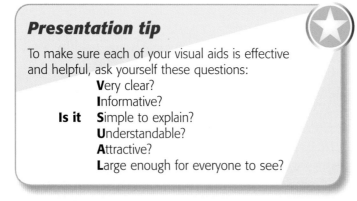

How do people watch movies at home?

3 — Venn diagram: online 33%, both 27%, on TV/DVD 40%

What are popular weekend activities for students?

shopping	10%
hanging out with friends	54%
working	20%
spending time with family	12%
4 studying	4%

B 🔘 10 What types of visual aids are used in Exercise A? Circle the correct type. Then listen and check your answers.

1. As this *graph / pie chart* explains, 20 percent of students said they want to study in the United States.
2. As this *table / pie chart* illustrates, 25 percent of young people said they prefer pop music.
3. As this *graph / Venn diagram* shows, 33 percent of people said they watch movies online.
4. As this *table / Venn diagram* makes clear, 20 percent of students said they work on weekends.

Presentation tip

To make sure each of your visual aids is effective and helpful, ask yourself these questions:

	Very clear?
	Informative?
Is it	**S**imple to explain?
	Understandable?
	Attractive?
	Large enough for everyone to see?

2 Your turn

A Write one more sentence for each visual aid on page 28. Use language from the box.

Explaining visual aids

| As this | pie chart
graph
table
Venn diagram | shows, . . .
illustrates, . . .
explains, . . .
makes clear, . . . |

1. _____

2. _____

3. _____

4. _____

B Work in groups. Take turns reading your sentences from Exercise A. When possible, try to say the numbers in as many different ways as you can.

"As this graph shows, 33 percent, or one-third, of university students said they want to study English in the U.K."

C Look at the class survey you did for Exercise 3A on page 23. On a separate piece of paper, create a simple visual aid using the information from your survey. Make your visual aid as effective and helpful as possible.

D Work with a partner. Take turns presenting your visual aids.

"I did a survey to find out about transportation. As this pie chart illustrates . . ."

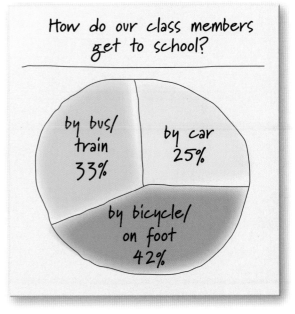

How do our class members get to school?

by bus/ train 33%

by car 25%

by bicycle/ on foot 42%

Now **present yourself!**

- **Turn to page 30.**
- **Prepare your presentation.**

Present yourself!

Give a presentation about a survey.

1 Brainstorming

A Choose a survey topic. Write it in the center of the brainstorming map. Then brainstorm survey questions you can ask about the topic. Use the examples in the box to help you.

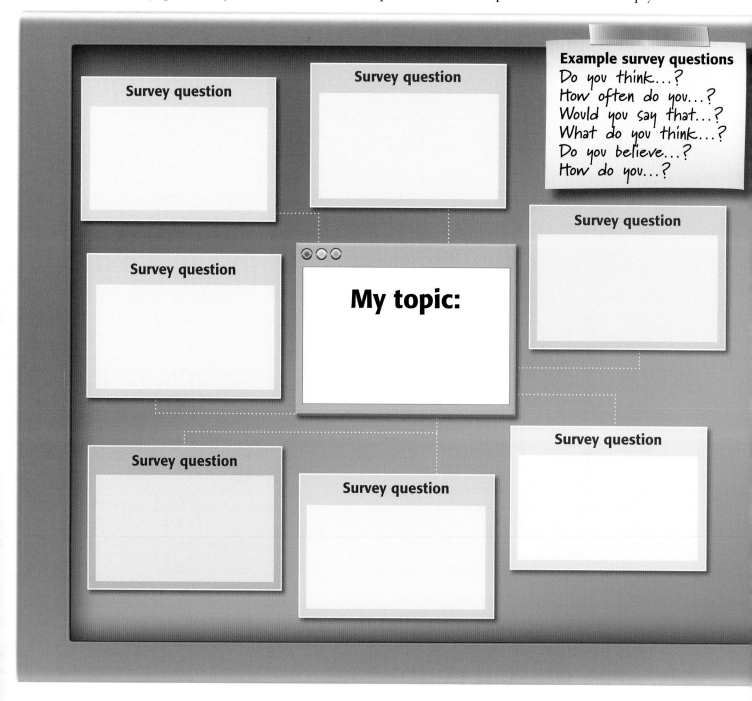

Example survey questions
Do you think...?
How often do you...?
Would you say that...?
What do you think...?
Do you believe...?
How do you...?

Survey question

Survey question

Survey question

Survey question

Survey question

My topic:

Survey question

Survey question

B Use your survey questions from Exercise A to interview a group of 8 to 10 people. Take notes on a separate piece of paper.

2 Organizing

Use your interview notes from Exercise 1B to complete the outline. Then make note cards from your outline and practice your presentation.

_____
(title)

I. Introduction

A. General information about the topic

_____

B. The aim of the survey

_____

II. Body

A. A description of the survey group

_____

B. A report of the survey results
- the questions asked
- the number of people and what they answered

_____
_____
_____
_____

III. Conclusion

A. A summary of the results

_____

B. My conclusion and recommendation

_____

3 Presenting

Give your presentation to the class.
Remember to use visual aids.

Don't forget to complete your self-evaluation on page 81 after your presentation.

3 Dream vacation

Topic focus

1 Vacations

A Look at the travel Web site. Where do you think these places are? Tell a partner.

Vacations

1. wildlife safari
2. beach resort vacation
3. historic sightseeing tour
4. outdoor adventure
5. rain forest ecotour
6. luxury cruise

B What kinds of people would enjoy the vacations in Exercise A? Match the pictures to these descriptions.

For people who . . .

_____ need to get away from it all and enjoy the sun and sand

_____ enjoy traveling in comfort and style

_____ like to visit world-famous attractions and learn about the past

__1__ want to observe animals in their natural habitats

_____ want an exciting, active vacation

_____ are concerned about the environment and want to help save endangered species

C Which vacation would you like to go on? Why? Tell the class.

"I'd like to go on the rain forest ecotour because . . ."

2 Travel preferences interview

A Read the interview questions and add one more. Then interview a partner and take notes on a separate piece of paper.

Travel preferences

1. Do you like to travel? Why or why not?
2. Do you prefer to travel in your own country or overseas? Why?
3. Do you prefer to be active or just relax when you're on vacation?
4. What types of activities do you like to do on vacation?
5. What's the most interesting place you've been to? Why?
6. What's one place in the world that you would love to visit?
7. _____

B Join another pair of students. Tell them three things about your partner's travel preferences.

"Jun loves to travel. He enjoys learning about other countries and . . . "

3 My perfect vacation

A What's your idea of the perfect vacation? Circle your choices or add your own ideas.

Perfect vacation planner

Region / location	Africa Europe North America Asia Oceania South America _____		
Type of place	beach city countryside mountains _____		
Length of stay	a weekend a week two or three weeks a month a few months _____		
Accommodations	bed-and-breakfast luxury hotel youth hostel cabin or bungalow tent _____		
Activities	do outdoor sports meet people relax learn something sightsee _____		

B Tell the class about your perfect vacation. Which choices are the most popular?

"My perfect vacation would be to go to Europe. I'd go to the countryside . . . "

Language focus

1 Vacation destinations

A Look at these vacation destinations. What do you know about the places? What do you think visitors can see or do there?

1. Borneo

2. Maui

3. Rome

B 🔊 11 Listen to travel agents describe these vacation destinations. Circle the correct information.

		Location	Description	Highlights
1.	Borneo	*Northeast / Southeast* Asia	*exotic / exciting*	rare *nightlife / wildlife*
2.	Maui	*northwest / northeast* of the Big Island	*beautiful / delightful*	fabulous *accommodations / activities*
3.	Rome	the *middle / south* of Italy	*scenic / romantic*	excellent *hotels / restaurants*

C Think of a popular vacation destination. Describe it to a partner. Don't name the place. Can your partner guess?

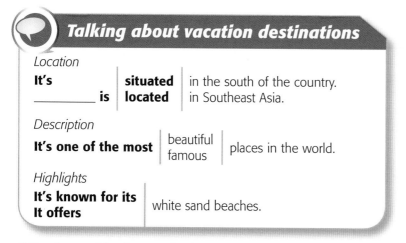

Talking about vacation destinations

Location

It's		**situated**	in the south of the country.
_____	**is**	**located**	in Southeast Asia.

Description

It's one of the most	beautiful	places in the world.
	famous	

Highlights

It's known for its		white sand beaches.
It offers		

"It's situated in the south of the country. It's one of the most beautiful places in the world. It's known for its white sand beaches. It offers . . . "

2 Activities and accommodations

A 12 Now listen to the travel agents describe the vacations. Check (✓) two activities and one accommodation type for each vacation.

Vacation	Activities	Accommodations
1. Borneo Jungle Ecotour	☐ hike through the jungle ☐ learn about plants and animals ☐ go on a night safari	☐ cabins ☐ tents
2. Maui Island Paradise	☐ go on an island cruise ☐ spend time shopping ☐ watch the sunset	☐ five-star resort ☐ beach bungalow
3. Journey Through Historic Rome	☐ learn about art and architecture ☐ eat at old restaurants ☐ visit the countryside	☐ bed-and-breakfast ☐ youth hostel

B Work with a partner. Take turns talking about the vacations in Exercise A. Which activities and accommodations would you like the most? Can you think of any others?

"I'd like to go on a night safari and stay in a cabin in Borneo. I'd also . . . "

3 Let's go!

A Think about the vacation destination you chose in Exercise 1C on page 34. Write two activities visitors can do there and one accommodation type on a separate piece of paper.

B Work in groups. Take turns talking about the activities and accommodations at your destination. Which ones would you like to try?

Talking about activities and accommodations

Activities

You can		relax on the beach.
You'll	**be able to** **have a chance to** **have an opportunity to**	ride an elephant.

Accommodations

You'll	**stay** **spend** four	**nights** **days**	**in a** beach bungalow.

"In Phuket, Thailand, you can relax on the beach, and you'll have a chance to ride an elephant. You'll stay . . . "

Organization focus

1 | Sam's dream vacation

A Look at the picture of Sam's dream vacation. How would you describe the place? What activities do you think visitors can do there?

B Read Sam's brainstorming notes for his presentation about his dream vacation. Check (✓) the eight topics he included in his outline on page 37.

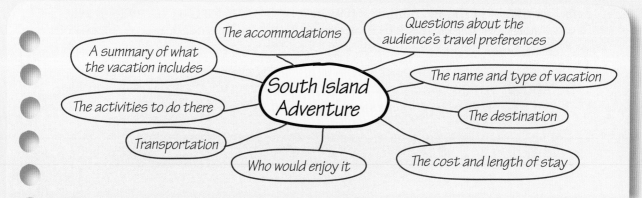

C Read Sam's additional notes for his presentation. Then use his notes to complete the outline on page 37.

- bed-and-breakfast
- near Australia in the Pacific Ocean
- Do you want to experience exotic cultures?

- eight nights
- perfect for people who want an exciting, active vacation
- go whale watching, swim with dolphins

2 Sam's outline

🔊 13 Listen to Sam's presentation. Check the notes you added from Exercise 1C on page 36.

South Island Adventure

I.   Introduction

    A. Questions about the audience's travel preferences

        1. Are you looking for some excitement?

        2. _____

    B. The name and type of vacation

        1. South Island Adventure

        2. an outdoor nature trek

    C. Who would enjoy it: _____

II. Body

    A. The destination

        1. the location: _____

        2. the description: one of the most fascinating places in the world

        3. the highlights: national parks, countryside, plants, wildlife, mountain views, ocean

    B. The activities to do there

        1. hike, explore caves and forests, learn about wildlife, see the kiwi bird

        2. experience Maori culture, paddle in canoe, visit meetinghouse

        3. _____

    C. The accommodations

        1. four-star hotel

        2. _____

III. Conclusion

    A. The cost and length of stay

        1. $1,200

        2. _____

    B. A summary of what the vacation includes

        1. outdoor activities

        2. natural scenery

        3. opportunity to explore the great outdoors

Presentation focus

1 Introduction

Notice the information Sam included in his introduction on page 39. Guess the missing words.

> ▶ Questions about the audience's travel preferences
>
> *Are you looking for some excitement?*   *Do you want to experience exotic cultures?*
>
> ▶ The name and type of vacation
>
> ▶ Who would enjoy it
>
> *This (vacation) is perfect for people who . . .*

2 Body

Notice the information Sam included in his introduction on page 39. Guess the missing words.

> ▶ The destination
>
> • the location
> • the description
> • the highlights
>
> ▶ The activities to do there
>
> ▶ The accommodations

3 Conclusion

Notice the information Sam included in his introduction on page 39. Guess the missing words.

> ▶ The cost and length of stay
>
> *The cost is $1,200 for eight nights.*
>
> ▶ A summary of what the vacation includes
>
> *This vacation includes . . .*

4 Sam's presentation

13   Listen to Sam's presentation. Check your guesses.

South Island Adventure

Introduction

Are you looking for some excitement? Do you want to experience exotic cultures? If your answer is yes, then I have the perfect vacation for you. It's the South Island Adventure, an outdoor _____ trek. This is perfect for people who want an _____ , active vacation.

Body

The South Island of New Zealand is located near Australia in the beautiful Pacific Ocean. It's one of the _____ fascinating places in the world. The South Island is _____ for its national parks, picturesque countryside, and exotic plants and wildlife. It also _____ stunning mountain views and clear blue ocean water.

On this trip, you _____ hike through Kahurangi National Park, which is situated in the northwest part of the South Island. You'll be _____ to explore deep caves and rich forests. You can learn about the amazing wildlife, including birds and insects that are found nowhere else in the world. You'll have a _____ to see New Zealand's national symbol, the kiwi bird, too! You'll also have an _____ to experience ancient Maori culture while paddling on a river in a traditional Maori canoe, and you can visit a traditional Maori meetinghouse. On your last day, you'll be _____ to go whale watching and swim with dolphins.

The accommodations on this trip will be unforgettable. On the first and last nights, you'll stay in a luxurious four-star _____ in Christchurch. Then, during the trek, you'll spend six nights in a cozy bed-and-breakfast near the park, with all meals included. New Zealand is known for its friendly people, and the family you'll stay with will make you feel very welcome.

Conclusion

Does this sound like a dream vacation? I think it does! The cost is $1,200 for eight nights. This vacation includes seven days of educational outdoor _____ and breathtaking natural _____ . It's a wonderful opportunity to explore the great outdoors. So, what are you waiting for? It's time to go on a South Island Adventure!

Presentation skills focus

1 Lead-in questions

Create curiosity and interest in your presentation by asking the audience lead-in questions about their preferences, needs, and experiences related to the topic.

Match the pictures to the questions below. (There is one extra question.)

_____ Do you need a break from work?

_____ Are you tired of crowded beaches?

_____ Do you want to escape to a tropical paradise?

_____ Do you love vacations that are full of outdoor adventure?

_____ Do you want to eat gourmet meals every night?

_____ Are you fed up with hotels that aren't like the brochure photos?

_____ Are you looking for a fun vacation for the whole family?

Presentation tip

- When you ask lead-in questions, you don't need to wait for the audience to answer you. Just ask the question, wait one second, and then ask the next question.
- Remember that with *Yes / No* questions, your intonation rises at the end.

2 Your turn

A Write one more lead-in question for each picture on page 40.

> ### Lead-in questions
>
> Are you fed up with . . . ?   Are you tired of . . . ?   Do you need . . . ?
> Are you looking for . . . ?   Do you love . . . ?   Do you want . . . ?

1. _____

2. _____

3. _____

4. _____

5. _____

6. _____

B Work with a partner. Take turns asking your lead-in questions from Exercise A. Don't ask them in order. Can your partner guess the picture?

"Are you fed up with working too much?"

C Look at the example introductions from two presentations about vacation destinations. Write two lead-in questions for each one.

1. _____

   _____

   If your answer is yes, then I have the perfect vacation for you. It's the Borneo jungle ecotour. This vacation is for people who want an action-packed travel experience.

2. _____

   _____

   If so, then the Maui island paradise vacation is for you. This is perfect for people who want to get away from it all.

D Work with a partner. Take turns reading the introductions in Exercise C aloud. Practice the timing and intonation of the lead-in questions.

Now **present yourself!**

- **Turn to page 42.**
- **Prepare your presentation.**

Present yourself!

1 Brainstorming

Choose a destination for your dream vacation. Write it in the center of the brainstorming map. Then add as many details as you can for each brainstorming topic.

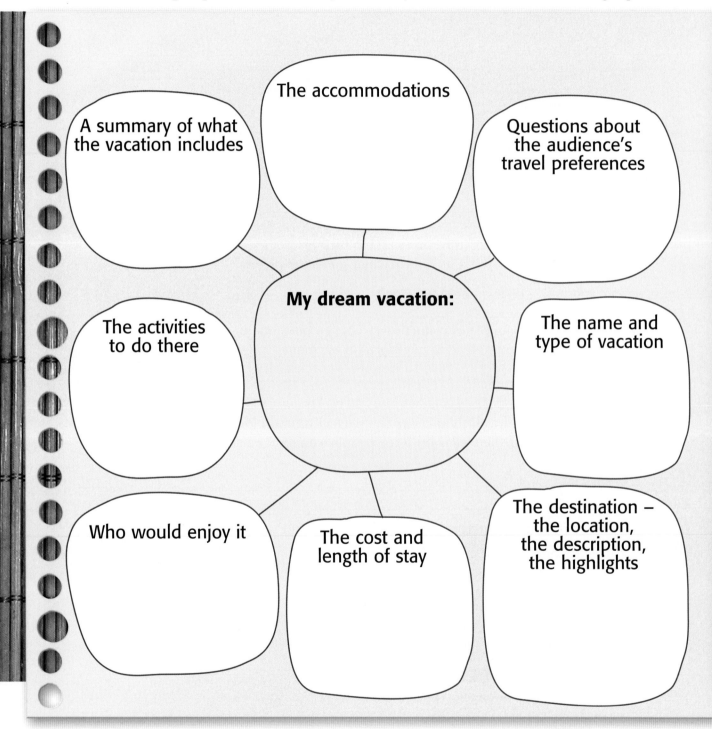

The accommodations

A summary of what the vacation includes

Questions about the audience's travel preferences

My dream vacation:

The activities to do there

The name and type of vacation

Who would enjoy it

The cost and length of stay

The destination – the location, the description, the highlights

2 Organizing

Use your brainstorming notes from Exercise 1 to complete the outline.
Then make note cards from your outline and practice your presentation.

(title)

I. Introduction

    A. Questions about the audience's travel preferences

    _____

    B. The name and type of vacation

    _____

    C. Who would enjoy it

    _____

II. Body

    A. The destination – the location, the description, the highlights

    _____

    B. The activities to do there

    _____

    C. The accommodations

    _____

III. Conclusion

    A. The cost and length of stay

    _____

    B. A summary of what the vacation includes

    _____

---

3 Presenting

Give your presentation to the class.
Remember to use lead-in questions.

> Don't forget to complete your self-evaluation on page 82 after your presentation.

4 How the world works

Topic focus

1 Trivia quiz

A Circle your answers to the trivia quiz. Then compare answers with a partner. (You can check your answers at the bottom of the quiz.)

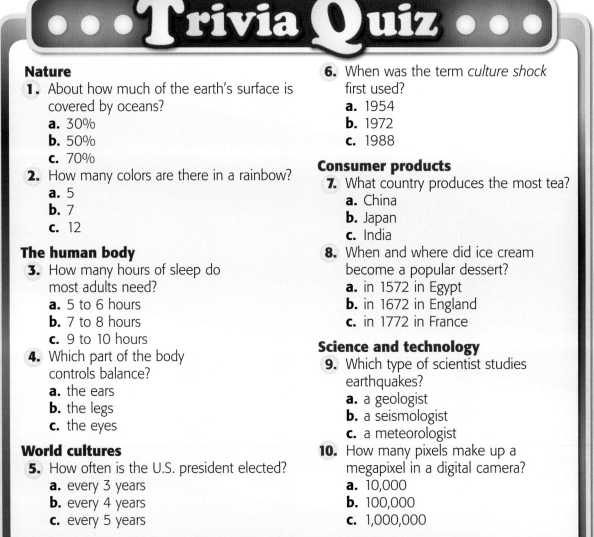

Trivia Quiz

Nature

1. About how much of the earth's surface is covered by oceans?
   a. 30%
   b. 50%
   c. 70%

2. How many colors are there in a rainbow?
   a. 5
   b. 7
   c. 12

The human body

3. How many hours of sleep do most adults need?
   a. 5 to 6 hours
   b. 7 to 8 hours
   c. 9 to 10 hours

4. Which part of the body controls balance?
   a. the ears
   b. the legs
   c. the eyes

World cultures

5. How often is the U.S. president elected?
   a. every 3 years
   b. every 4 years
   c. every 5 years

6. When was the term *culture shock* first used?
   a. 1954
   b. 1972
   c. 1988

Consumer products

7. What country produces the most tea?
   a. China
   b. Japan
   c. India

8. When and where did ice cream become a popular dessert?
   a. in 1572 in Egypt
   b. in 1672 in England
   c. in 1772 in France

Science and technology

9. Which type of scientist studies earthquakes?
   a. a geologist
   b. a seismologist
   c. a meteorologist

10. How many pixels make up a megapixel in a digital camera?
    a. 10,000
    b. 100,000
    c. 1,000,000

Quiz answers: 1. c; 2. b; 3. b; 4. a; 5. b; 6. a; 7. a; 8. b; 9. b; 10. c.

B Write two more trivia quiz questions with answer choices on a separate piece of paper. Then ask your partner the questions.

"What is the highest mountain in the world? Is it Mount Kilimanjaro, Mount Fuji, or Mount Everest?"

2 Process topics

A Match each presentation in the conference schedule to one of the topics. (Some presentations may match more than one topic.) Then compare answers with a partner.

Topics

a. Consumer products   c. Nature   e. World cultures

b. The human body   d. Science and technology

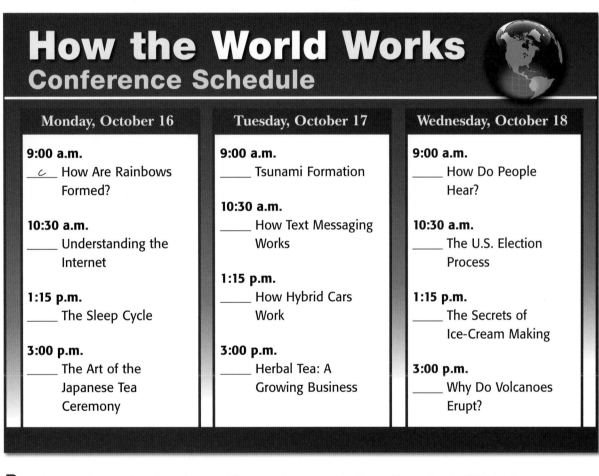

How the World Works
Conference Schedule

Monday, October 16	Tuesday, October 17	Wednesday, October 18
9:00 a.m. _c_ How Are Rainbows Formed?	**9:00 a.m.** ___ Tsunami Formation	**9:00 a.m.** ___ How Do People Hear?
10:30 a.m. ___ Understanding the Internet	**10:30 a.m.** ___ How Text Messaging Works	**10:30 a.m.** ___ The U.S. Election Process
1:15 p.m. ___ The Sleep Cycle	**1:15 p.m.** ___ How Hybrid Cars Work	**1:15 p.m.** ___ The Secrets of Ice-Cream Making
3:00 p.m. ___ The Art of the Japanese Tea Ceremony	**3:00 p.m.** ___ Herbal Tea: A Growing Business	**3:00 p.m.** ___ Why Do Volcanoes Erupt?

B Join another pair of students. Choose three topics from Exercise A. Write the topics and one new title for each presentation on a separate piece of paper.

> Nature — How Does Thunder Happen?
>
> World cultures — University Systems in the United States and Europe
>
> Science and technology — Understanding Digital Photography

C Share your presentation titles with the class. What do your classmates know about the processes?

"Our first title is 'How Does Thunder Happen?'"

    "I know! Thunder happens when warm air . . . "

Language focus

1 Introducing a process presentation

A 🔘 14 Listen to Kazu and Tami introduce their process presentations. Check (✓) the correct presentation titles.

1. Kazu

   ☐ Curing Sleep Disorders

   ☐ Why We Dream

   ☐ The Sleep Cycle

2. Tami

   ☐ Understanding Ocean Tides

   ☐ Tsunami Formation

   ☐ How Water Pollution Occurs

B 🔘 14 Listen again. Check (✓) the three pieces of information each person will discuss.

1. Kazu

   ☐ what the stages of sleep are called

   ☐ how sleep disorders are treated

   ☐ when dreams are created

   ☐ how health is influenced

   ☐ how the brain is affected

2. Tami

   ☐ which places are affected

   ☐ how people are rescued

   ☐ what kinds of damage are caused

   ☐ how the waves are formed

   ☐ how ocean animals are affected

C Work with a partner. Imagine you are Kazu or Tami. Take turns introducing your process presentation.

Introducing a process presentation

In this	presentation, talk,	I'll	explain discuss go over	what the stages of sleep are called. which places are affected.

"In this presentation, I'll explain . . . "

2 | How does it happen?

A 🔘 15 Match the stages of the processes to what happens during each stage.
Then listen and check your guesses.

The stages	What happens
1. a. drowsiness	____ The brain waves are slowed.
b. light sleep	____ The heart rate is lowered.
c. deep sleep	____ Dreaming begins.
d. REM sleep	_a_ The eyes first close.
2. a. There is an underwater earthquake.	____ Houses and buildings are destroyed.
b. Layers of earth are pushed together.	____ The waves gain speed and strength.
c. Waves are created.	____ The ocean floor moves suddenly.
d. The waves hit shore.	____ The water level rises slightly.

B Work with a partner. Take turns explaining the processes in Exercise A.

Explaining a process

Named stages

The	**first** **second** **next** **final**	**stage is** the drowsiness stage.

Unnamed stages

In the first stage, there is an underwater earthquake.

What happens

This is when **During this stage,** **At this point,**	the eyes first close. the ocean floor moves suddenly.

C Change partners. Then take turns explaining the process below.

How newspapers are made

The stages	What happens
1 Reporters investigate facts. ▷	Stories are researched, and people are interviewed.
2 Stories are written. ▷	Stories are typed into a computer.
3 Stories are edited. ▷	Stories are corrected and arranged on the pages.
4 Stories are printed. ▷	The pages are put on a printing press.

"In this talk, I'll explain how newspapers are made. In the first stage,
reporters investigate facts. This is when . . . "

1 Nicole's process presentation

A Look at the picture for Nicole's process presentation. Where do you think this is? What is happening?

B Read Nicole's brainstorming notes for her presentation about a process. Check (✔) the eight topics she included in her outline on page 49.

Coffee Manufacturing: From Bean to Cup

A preview of the presentation

First stage: growing and harvesting

Second stage: processing

An interesting fact about the process

My favorite type of coffee

Third stage: roasting

Recommendations for further research

Final stage: grinding and brewing

A review of all the stages of the process

C Read Nicole's additional notes for her presentation. Then use her notes to complete the outline on page 49.

- beans are dried, sorted, put into sacks for shipping

- beans are heated to 240°C in roasting machine

- go over how raw beans are processed

- coffee cherries are picked by hand or machine

- grinding and brewing

- whole beans are crushed, mixed with hot water

2) Nicole's outline

16 Listen to Nicole's presentation. Check the notes you added from Exercise 1C on page 48.

Coffee Manufacturing: From Bean to Cup

I. Introduction

    A. An interesting fact about the process: second-most traded product in the world

    B. A preview of the presentation

        1. explain how beans are grown and harvested

        2. _____

        3. take questions when I'm finished

II. Body

    A. First stage: growing and harvesting

        1. trees produce small berries called coffee cherries

        2. after five years, coffee cherries are ready to be harvested

        3. _____

    B. Second stage: processing

        1. red coffee cherries are changed into green coffee beans

        2. outer fruit is removed from coffee cherries, only seeds (beans) are left

        3. _____

    C. Third stage: roasting

        1. _____

        2. length of time determines color, richness

    D. Final stage: grinding and brewing

        1. _____

        2. different methods, depending on strength of coffee

III. Conclusion

    A. A review of all the stages of the process

        1. growing and harvesting

        2. processing

        3. roasting

        4. _____

    B. Recommendations for further research: Coffee: A Cultural History from Around the World by Ed Milton

Presentation focus

1 Introduction

Notice the information Nicole included in her introduction on page 51. Guess the missing words.

> ▶ An interesting fact about the process
>
> *Did you know that . . . ?*   *Many people don't know that . . .*
>
> ▶ A preview of the presentation
>
> • an introduction to the process
> • an invitation for audience questions
>
> *I'll be happy to take your questions when I'm finished.*

2 Body

Notice the information Nicole included in her body on page 51. Guess the missing words.

> ▶ An explanation of the process
>
> • the stages and what happens

3 Conclusion

Notice the information Nicole included in her conclusion on page 51. Guess the missing words.

> ▶ A review of all the stages of the process
>
> *That completes the coffee-manufacturing process . . .*
>
> ▶ Recommendations for further research
>
> *For those of you who'd like to find out more, I recommend . . .*
>
> *If you'd like to learn more, you can . . .*

4 Nicole's presentation

🔵 16 Listen to Nicole's presentation. Check your guesses.

Coffee Manufacturing: From Bean to Cup

Introduction

These days we're never far from a coffee shop. There's one on almost every street corner. Did you know that coffee is the second-most traded _____ in the world, after oil? _____ this talk, I'll explain how coffee beans are grown and harvested, and I'll go _____ how the raw beans are processed and turned into the delicious drink many of us enjoy every morning. I'll be happy to take your questions when I'm finished. OK, let's get started.

Body

The first stage of coffee manufacturing is the growing and harvesting stage. _____ this stage, the coffee trees produce small red berries called coffee cherries. About five years after a new tree is planted, the coffee cherries are ready to be harvested. At this _____ , the coffee cherries are picked either by hand or machine.

The second stage is the processing stage. This is _____ the red coffee cherries are changed into green coffee beans. During this _____ , the outer fruit is removed from the coffee cherries, so only the coffee seeds, or beans, are left. The beans are then dried, sorted, and put into cloth sacks for shipping.

The next stage, or _____ stage, is the roasting stage. During this stage, the beans are placed in a roasting machine and heated to around 240 degrees Celsius. The length of roasting time determines the beans' color and richness.

The _____ stage of coffee manufacturing is the grinding and brewing stage. This is when the whole beans are crushed into a powder and mixed with hot water to make a cup of coffee. There are different methods of grinding and brewing, depending on how strong you want the coffee to taste.

Conclusion

That completes the coffee-manufacturing process: growing and _____ the coffee cherries, processing the fruit, roasting the beans, and finally, _____ and brewing the coffee. For those of you who'd like to find out more, I recommend reading <u>Coffee: A Cultural History from Around the World</u> by Ed Milton. Thank you. We have a few minutes left. I'll be glad to take your questions now.

Presentation skills focus

Inviting audience questions

When you give a presentation, there are two ways to handle audience questions:

- Invite the audience to ask questions during the presentation.
- Leave time for audience questions after the presentation.

During your introduction, tell the audience when you'd like them to ask questions.

Look at the sentences for inviting audience questions. Which are used for inviting questions during the presentation? after the presentation? Write *D* (during) or *A* (after) for each one.

A	I'll be happy to take your questions when I'm finished.
	Feel free to interrupt me if you have questions.
	If you have questions, please ask them at any time.
	I'll take questions after the presentation.
	Please hold your questions until the end.
	Please stop me at any time if you have questions.

Presentation tip

Follow these simple tips when answering audience questions:
- Welcome the question. You can say, "Good question" or "Thank you for bringing that up."
- Be an echo. Repeat the question if the questioner has a soft voice.
- When answering a question, K.I.S.S. – keep it short and simple.
- Don't panic. If you don't know the answer to a question, say, "I don't know, but I'll find out and get back to you."

2 Your turn

A Complete the introductions with sentences for inviting audience questions from page 52. Use the word given to choose an appropriate sentence. (There is more than one correct answer.)

1. In this presentation, I'll go over the sleep cycle and what really happens when we sleep.

   (during) _____

2. In this talk, I'll discuss the process of how tsunamis are formed and the kinds of damage they cause.

   (after) _____

3. In this presentation, I'll go over the stages of the Japanese tea ceremony and what they mean.

   (during) _____

4. In this talk, I'll explain how newspapers are made and how technology has changed this process.

   (after) _____

5. In this presentation, I'll discuss how hybrid cars work and how they can save you money.

   (after) _____

6. In this talk, I'll explain how people hear and why hearing is one of our most important senses.

   (during) _____

B Work with a partner. Take turns reading the examples in Exercise A aloud. Practice inviting audience questions.

C Change partners. Take turns introducing the processes and inviting audience questions.

How ice cream is made	How text messaging works	How cash machines work
The U.S. election process	Why volcanoes erupt	The coffee-manufacturing process

"In this presentation, I'll explain how ice cream is made.
I'll be happy to take your questions when I'm finished."

Now **present yourself!**

- **Turn to page 54.**
- **Prepare your presentation.**

Present yourself!

Give a presentation about how something works.

1 Brainstorming

Choose a process. Write it at the top of the brainstorming map. Then find out as much information as you can about it. Use books, magazines, the Internet, or other sources. Write as many details as you can for each brainstorming topic.

My process: _____

A preview of the presention

- an introduction to the process

- an invitation for audience questions

Recommendations for further research

A review of all the stages of the process

An explanation of the process

An interesting fact about the process

- the stages and what happens

2 Organizing

Use your brainstorming notes from Exercise 1 to complete the outline.
Then make note cards from your outline and practice your presentation.

_____ (title)

I. Introduction
   A. An interesting fact about the process

   _____

   B. A preview of the presentation
      • an introduction to the process

   _____

      • an invitation for audience questions

   _____

II. Body
   An explanation of the process
   • the stages and what happens

   _____

   _____

   _____

   _____

   _____

III. Conclusion
   A. A review of all the stages of the process

   _____

   _____

   B. Recommendations for further research

   _____

3 Presenting

Give your presentation to the class.
Remember to invite audience questions.

Don't forget to complete your self-evaluation on page 83 after your presentation.

5 *In my opinion*

Topic focus

1 Issues

A Look at the banners and signs. Can you guess what each issue is?

Improve our kids' schools!

Ban cell phone use!

Save our forests!

Spend time with your family today!

Exercise your **right** to vote!

No junk food in schools!

B Complete the chart with issues from the box. Then think of one more for each category.

Issues			
✓ fast food	marriage	recycling	university tuition
global warming	medical research	school uniforms	violence on TV
Internet use	raising children	taxes	volunteer work

Education	Human relationships	Media and technology
_____	_____	_____
_____	_____	_____

The environment	Lifestyle and health	Society and politics
_____	*fast food*	_____
_____	_____	_____

C Work with a partner. Which issues in Exercise B do you have strong opinions about?

"I have strong opinions about fast food and . . . "

2   Opinions survey

A Complete the survey. Read each sentence. Then check (✓) your opinion.

	agree	disagree	not sure
The Internet makes life better.			
Everyone should learn English.			
People shouldn't eat meat.			
Advertising aimed at children should be banned.			
Recycling should be required by law.			
People should wait until age 30 to get married.			
Watching TV harms young people.			
All cars should have hybrid engines.			
Only very wealthy people should pay taxes.			
All high school students should wear school uniforms.			
Traveling is more educational than going to school.			
All university students should do volunteer work.			

B Work in groups. Take turns sharing your opinions. Explain the reasons for your choices.

"I agree that the Internet makes life better because it's so easy to get information. What do you think?"

3   My opinions

A Choose two issues that you have strong opinions about. Then complete the chart.

Issue	Opinion	Reason
Education	Everyone should attend university.	It's important for success in life.
1.		
2.		

B Tell a partner your opinions. Explain your reasons. Does your partner agree?

"I have strong opinions about education. For example, I think everyone should attend university because it's important for success in life."

     "I don't think so. I think . . . "

Language focus

1 Expressing opinions

A Look at the pictures. Each one shows two sides of an issue. What do you think the issues are? Compare your ideas with a partner.

B 🔊 17 Listen to Alex, Elena, and Lisa express their opinions about these issues. Check (✓) the correct pictures in Exercise A that show their opinions.

C 🔊 17 Listen again. Check (✓) the two reasons Alex, Elena, and Lisa give for their opinions.

1. Alex	☐ It saves money.	☐ It's fashionable.	☐ It improves schoolwork.
2. Elena	☐ It keeps kids busy.	☐ It's not controlled.	☐ It can be dangerous.
3. Lisa	☐ It's educational.	☐ It's rewarding.	☐ It's enjoyable.

D Work in groups. Each group member chooses one of the issues in Exercise A. Take turns relating your issue to your group members. Be sure to express your opinion.

💬 Relating an issue and expressing an opposing opinion

Relating an issue to the audience
Many of you say that you don't like school uniforms.
Most people believe that the Internet can be a learning tool for kids.
We all have busy schedules.

Expressing an opposing opinion

However, But	I (don't)	think believe	that	school uniforms	should shouldn't	be required.
	in my opinion, I feel strongly that					

"Many of you say that you don't like school uniforms. However, I think that school uniforms should be required, because . . . "

58 Unit 5

2 Supporting opinions

A 🔘 18 Check (✓) the three pieces of information you think Alex, Elena, and Lisa use to support their opinions. Then listen and check your guesses.

1. Alex
  ☐ Some teens spend up to $100 a month on clothes.
  ☐ Most students prefer wearing uniforms.
  ☐ Paying attention to fashion negatively affects schoolwork.
  ☐ Differences between social groups are less obvious.

2. Elena
  ☐ Many kids think it's OK to share personal information.
  ☐ Supervising kids' Internet use can help parents worry less.
  ☐ It can be expensive.
  ☐ It's a way to do something together with your kids.

3. Lisa
  ☐ Only 10 percent of people volunteer.
  ☐ It's a valuable opportunity to get work experience.
  ☐ A friend had trouble finding a job.
  ☐ University students don't need part-time jobs.

B Work with a partner. Think of an issue you have a strong opinion about. Write your opinion and general information or facts that support it on a separate piece of paper.

C Work in groups. Take turns sharing and supporting your opinions. Do your classmates agree or disagree? Why?

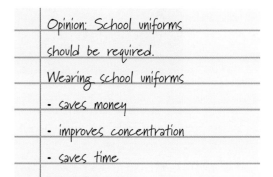

Opinion: School uniforms
should be required.
Wearing school uniforms
- saves money
- improves concentration
- saves time

💬 Supporting opinions

General information and facts
Did you know that wearing school uniforms saves money?

It's a fact that		
According to	**experts, researchers,**	young people spend a lot of money on clothes.
An article I read said that		only 10 percent of people volunteer.

Examples and anecdotes
In my experience, supervising kids' Internet use can help parents worry less.
Here's an example that supports my opinion.

"Did you know that wearing school uniforms saves money?
An article I read said that . . . "

Organization focus

1 Chris's persuasive presentation

A Look at this picture from an article Chris read for his persuasive presentation. What issue do you think he'll talk about? Can you guess his opinion?

B Read Chris's brainstorming notes for his persuasive presentation. Check (✓) the eight topics he included in his outline on page 61.

People Should Stop Eating Meat

Supporting information about cost
A statement relating the issue to the audience
My opposing opinion
Statements to persuade the audience

The number of vegetarians in this country
Supporting information about health
The reasons for my opinion
A summary of my opinion and the reasons
Supporting information about helping the environment

C Read Chris's additional notes for his presentation. Then use his notes to complete the outline on page 61.

- helps the environment
- I lost five kilos, have more energy, feel great
- meat is most expensive part of diet

- Everyone should become a vegetarian.
- wasn't easy, but made the right choice, and hope you will, too
- about 25 percent of rain forest destroyed in Central America since 1960

2) Chris's outline

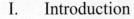 19   Listen to Chris's presentation. Check the notes you added from
Exercise 1C on page 60.

People Should Stop Eating Meat

I.   Introduction

   A. A statement relating the issue to the audience: We all enjoy a good meal,
and I know that for many of you, that includes eating meat.

   B. My opposing opinion

      1. People should stop eating meat.

      2. _____

   C. The reasons for my opinion

      1. is good for health

      2. saves money

      3. _____

II. Body

   A. Supporting information about health

      1. vegetarian diet is healthier

      2. people who eat meat have higher rates of heart disease

      3. _____

   B. Supporting information about cost

      1. _____

      2. meat products cost three times as much as same amount of vegetables

   C. Supporting information about helping the environment

      1. meat industries cut down rain forest in Central and South America

      2. _____

III. Conclusion

   A. A summary of my opinion and the reasons

      1. vegetarian diet is the best choice

      2. you'll be healthier, save money, help the environment

   B. Statements to persuade the audience

      1. not easy to give up something you enjoy

      2. _____

Presentation focus

1 Introduction

Notice the information Chris included in his introduction on page 63. Guess the missing words.

▶ A statement relating the issue to the audience

▶ His opposing opinion

▶ The reasons for his opinion

2 Body

Notice the information Chris included in his body on page 63. Guess the missing words.

▶ Information to support his opinion (supporting information)

- general information and facts
- examples and anecdotes

3 Conclusion

Notice the information Chris included in his conclusion on page 63. Guess the missing words.

▶ A summary of his opinion and the reasons
   In conclusion, I believe . . .

▶ Statements to persuade the audience
   I know it's not easy to . . .   *I made the right choice, and I hope you will, too.*

4 Chris's presentation

 19   Listen to Chris's presentation. Check your guesses.

People Should Stop Eating Meat

Introduction

We all enjoy a good meal, and I know that for many of you, that includes eating meat. Hamburgers are tasty, and there's nothing like a good steak or some fried chicken. However, I believe that people should stop eating meat. Yes. In my _____ , everyone should become a vegetarian! There are three good reasons to support this view. It's good for your health, and it _____ money. Also, eating a vegetarian diet _____ the environment.

Body

First, let's consider health. It's a _____ that a vegetarian diet is healthier than one that includes meat. _____ to health experts, people who eat meat have higher rates of heart disease. In my _____ , eating a vegetarian diet can make a big difference. I stopped eating meat a year ago, and I lost about five kilos in the first two months. I now have a lot more energy, and I feel great about myself.

Now let's think about money. Did you _____ that meat is the most expensive part of your diet? That's right. Meat products cost around three times as much as an equal amount of vegetables. Just imagine how much money you'd save by cutting meat from your shopping list.

Another reason to support a vegetarian diet is to help the environment, such as the rain forest. An _____ I _____ said that some meat industries cut down large sections of the rain forest in Central and South America in order to create more land to raise animals for meat. In fact, about 25 percent of the rain forest in Central America has been destroyed since 1960. Our planet needs the rain forests, and cutting them down will hurt everyone.

Conclusion

In conclusion, I believe that a vegetarian _____ is the best choice. You'll be healthier, you'll save a lot of money, and you'll be helping the _____ . Of course, I know it's not easy to give up something you _____ . It wasn't easy for me at first. But I made the right choice, and I hope you will, too – for yourself and for the world! Thank you.

Presentation skills focus

1 Emphasizing an opposing opinion

When you give a persuasive presentation, use emphasis to make it clear that you hold an opposing opinion.

A 🔘 20   Listen. Notice the words that are emphasized to show the speakers' opposing opinions.

... However, in **my** opinion, uniforms **should** be required for all students.

1

... But I don't think that young kids should use the Internet unless a parent is with them.

2

... However, I feel **strongly** that university students should do volunteer work.

Be a Volunteer. Help!

3

B 🔘 21   Listen to people express their opinions. Complete the sentences.

1. Many people say that recycling should be a personal choice. ___*However*___ , ___*I*___ ___*believe*___ that recycling should be required by law.

2. We all understand that paying taxes is the duty of all citizens. _____ _____ _____ _____ , only very wealthy people should pay taxes.

3. We all know that TV advertising aimed at children is very effective. _____ _____ _____ _____ that advertising aimed at children should be banned.

4. Most people think that school is the best place for young people to get an education. _____ , _____ _____ _____ , traveling is more educational than going to school.

Presentation tip

You can emphasize your opinion by using body language.
- When relating an issue to the audience, gesture toward the people.
- When expressing your opinion, gesture toward yourself to emphasize that you're explaining your own opinion.

2 Your turn

A 🔘 22   Read the example from a persuasive presentation. Then listen and circle the word that is emphasized in each underlined phrase.

> None of us likes the idea of giving up our cars. However, I feel (strongly) that people should stop driving cars. According to experts, we're using more oil than ever before, and pollution from cars hurts the environment. Many people believe that ethanol will power our cars in the future. But I don't believe that ethanol is the solution. In my opinion, we need to make lifestyle changes. I think that people should use public transportation more, and many of us can walk or ride a bike to work or school. In my experience, it isn't too hard to give up driving.

B   Work with a partner. Take turns reading the example in Exercise A aloud. Practice emphasizing the words that make the speaker's opinions clear.

C   With your partner, choose an issue to discuss. Take opposing opinions on the issue. Then write sentences to support your opinion. Use the language on page 58.

The issue: _____

Relating the issue to my audience:

1. _____

2. _____

My opposing opinion:

1. _____

2. _____

D   Take turns sharing your opinions in Exercise C. Use emphasis to make your opinion clear.

"Some people feel anxious at the thought of going abroad to do a homestay. But I believe that doing a homestay is the best way to learn another language. In my . . ."

Now **present yourself!**

- **Turn to page 66.**
- **Prepare your presentation.**

Present yourself! Give a presentation about an important issue.

1 Brainstorming

Choose an issue you feel strongly about. Write it in the center of the brainstorming map. Then add as many details as you can for each brainstorming topic.

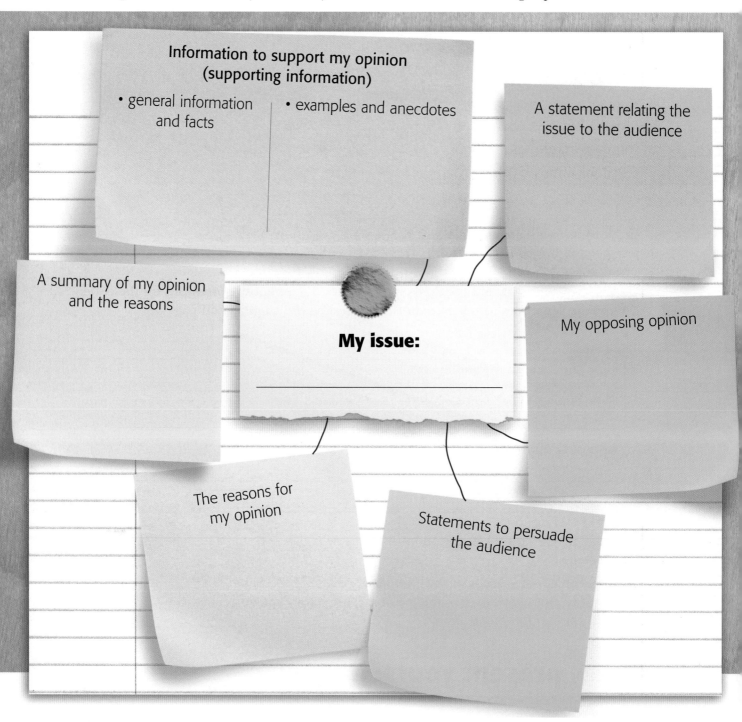

Information to support my opinion (supporting information)

• general information and facts

• examples and anecdotes

A statement relating the issue to the audience

A summary of my opinion and the reasons

My issue:
_____

My opposing opinion

The reasons for my opinion

Statements to persuade the audience

2 Organizing

Use your brainstorming notes from Exercise 1 to complete the outline.
Then make note cards from your outline and practice your presentation.

_____
(title)

I. **Introduction**

   A. A statement relating the issue to the audience

   _____

   B. My opposing opinion

   _____

   C. The reasons for my opinion

   _____

II. **Body**

   Information to support my opinion (supporting information)

   • general information and facts

   • examples and anecdotes

   _____

   _____

   _____

   _____

III. **Conclusion**

   A. A summary of my opinion and the reasons

   _____

   B. Statements to persuade the audience

   _____

3 Presenting

Give your presentation to the class.
Remember to emphasize your opposing opinion.

Don't forget to complete your self-evaluation on page 84 after your presentation.

6 *In the news*

1 News headlines

A Look at the pictures from stories in the news. What do you think the stories are about?

"I think this story is about planes and . . . "

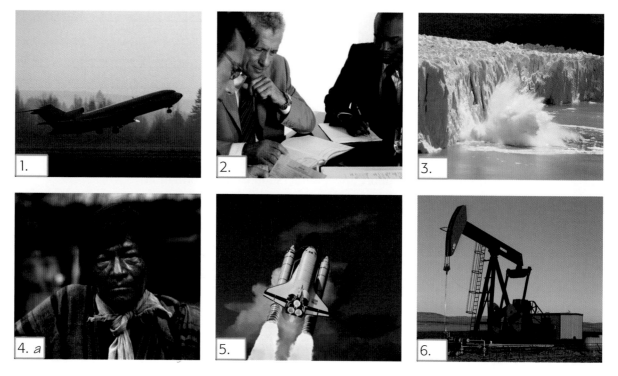

B Match the headlines to the pictures in Exercise A. Then compare answers with a partner. (There is one extra headline.)

a. Amazonian Tribe Faces Extinction

d. Medical Breakthrough: Cure for Cancer

b. Space Travel: Is It Worth the Money?

e. How Safe Is Air Travel Today?

c. World Oil Prices Reach Record Levels

f. Global Warming: Earth Is in Danger

g. Where Are All the Female Executives?

C Which news stories are you most interested in? What would you like to know about them? Tell your partner.

"I'm interested in the story with the title 'Amazonian Tribe Faces Extinction.' I'd like to know . . . "

2 The news and you

A Check (✓) or write your own answers to questions about the news. Then share your answers with a partner.

1. How often do you watch or listen to the news?
    ☐ every day   ☐ once or twice a week
    ☐ three or four times a week ☐ _____

2. Where do you usually get the news?
    ☐ on the Internet   ☐ in the newspaper   ☐ _____
    ☐ on the radio   ☐ on TV

3. What kinds of news stories are you most interested in?
    ☐ business   ☐ health
    ☐ entertainment   ☐ international
    ☐ politics   ☐ sports
    ☐ science and technology ☐ _____

B Complete the chart with information about an interesting news story you know about.

News source (where I heard or saw the story)	Where and when the story happened	Topic (who or what the story is about)
on TV	in the United States last month	postcard sent 93 years ago finally arrived

C Join another pair of students. Take turns talking about your news stories. How would you describe your classmates' stories? Use words from the box.

Words to describe news stories			
astonishing	fascinating	moving	thought-provoking
disturbing	heartwarming	shocking	timely

"I saw this story on TV. It happened in the United States last month. A postcard sent 93 years ago finally arrived!"
   "Really? That's astonishing!"

Language focus

1 Introducing news stories

A Look at the headlines and pictures. What do you know about the stories?

Too Many People?	Are People Happy?	You Are What You Eat
1	2	3

B 23 Listen to Mei, Jeff, and Luis introduce the stories in Exercise A. Write *M* (Mei), *J* (Jeff), or *L* (Luis) in each column next to the words and phrases that they say.

News source	Topic	Presentation preview
_M_ magazine	____ fast-food warnings	____ summarize main points
____ radio	____ medical research	_M_ give my reaction
____ Internet	____ modern lifestyles	____ share your opinion
____ TV	_M_ population trends	____ share my ideas

C Work with a partner. Take turns introducing your news stories from page 69.

Introducing news stories

News source

I	read saw heard	a(n)	astonishing disturbing	article report story	on	the Internet. TV. the radio.

Topic

It	looked at talked about	a postcard sent 93 years ago that finally arrived.

Previewing the presentation

First, Today,	I'll I'm going to	outline summarize	the main points (of the	article). report). story).

Then I'll	give you my reaction. tell you how I feel about it.

At the end	you'll have a chance to share your opinion. I'll ask for your comments and opinions.

"I saw an astonishing story on TV. It talked about a postcard . . . "

2 The details

A 💿 24 Now listen to Mei, Jeff, and Luis explain their news stories. Check (✔) the detail they mention.

1. Mei   ☐ Some Asian countries have very low birthrates.
           ☐ Over one billion people live in China.

2. Jeff   ☐ Money becomes less important as people get older.
           ☐ Many women feel overwhelmed by the demands of work and family.

3. Luis   ☐ The government may put warnings on unhealthy foods.
           ☐ The government may raise taxes on unhealthy foods.

B 💿 24 Listen again. Check (✔) *true* or *false*.

			true	false
1.	Mei	The population went from five to six billion in 12 years.	☐	☐
2.	Jeff	Being active is one of the keys to happiness.	☐	☐
3.	Luis	Most officials don't support a fast-food tax.	☐	☐

3 Reality or fiction?

A Think of a news story you know about, or create your own. Then complete the chart.

Topic	Details
robots for the elderly	• robots for the elderly now available • look after elderly in place of busy family members

B Work in groups. Take turns talking about the details of your news stories.

Talking about details in news stories

According to the	article, report, story,	
The	article report story	said stated	that

robots for the elderly are available.

It went on to say that the robots will look after the elderly.

"I read an article in the newspaper. It talked about robots for elderly people. According to the article, . . . "

Organization focus

1 Mari's news story

A Look at the picture from Mari's news story. What do you think the topic of the story is? How do you think she describes it?

B Read Mari's brainstorming notes for her presentation about a news story. Check (✓) the nine topics she included in her outline on page 73.

Worlds Apart

A question for the audience to think about   My reaction to the news story

My trip to Africa   Details about what is being done

A preview of the presentation   An introduction to the news story

Details about world poverty   A surprising fact about the topic

An invitation for audience members   Details about education

to share their views

C Read Mari's additional notes for her presentation. Then use her notes to complete the outline on page 73.

- the topic: poverty in the world
- Half the world's population lives on less than $2 a day.
- nongovernmental organizations and charities are helping
- outline main points
- $10 billion is enough to put every child in school, but is less than one percent of what world spends on arms
- story is shocking, moving
- one in two children lives in poverty
- share your opinion at end

2 Mari's outline

25 Listen to Mari's presentation. Check the notes you added for Exercise 1C on page 72.

Worlds Apart

I.   Introduction

   A. A question for the audience to think about: Can you imagine living on $2 a day?

   B. A surprising fact about the topic: _____

   C. An introduction to the news story

       1. the news source: disturbing article in a newsmagazine

       2. _____

   D. A preview of the presentation

       1. _____

       2. tell you how I feel

       3. _____

II. Body

   A. Details about world poverty

       1. three richest people have more wealth than 48 poorest countries

       2. _____

       3. 27,000 children die every day from poverty

   B. Details about education

       1. one billion people entered 21st century unable to read or sign their names

       2. _____

   C. Details about what is being done

       1. _____

       2. businesses and corporations are helping, for example, Product Red

III. Conclusion

   A. My reaction to the news story

       1. _____

       2. made me hopeful when read about work of charity organizations

       3. if we all help, it'll make a difference

   B. An invitation for audience members to share their views: now, your views

Presentation focus

1 Introduction

Notice the information Mari included in her introduction on page 75. Guess the missing words.

▶ A question for the audience to think about

Think for a second.   *Can you imagine . . . ?*   *Suppose you . . .*

▶ A surprising fact about the topic

You may be surprised to hear that . . .

▶ An introduction to the news story

  • the news source
  • the topic

▶ A preview of the presentation

2 Body

Notice the information Mari included in her body on page 75. Guess the missing words.

▶ The details of the news story

3 Conclusion

Notice the information Mari included in her conclusion on page 75. Guess the missing words.

▶ Her reaction to the news story

I think this story is . . .   *It made me feel . . .*

▶ An invitation for audience members to share their views

Now I'd like to hear your views on . . .

4 Mari's presentation

 25   Listen to Mari's presentation. Check your guesses.

Worlds Apart

Introduction

Think for a second. Can you imagine living on two U.S. dollars a day? Well, you may be surprised to hear this. _____ the world's population – three billion people – lives on less than two dollars a day! The other day, I _____ a disturbing story in a newsmagazine. It _____ about poverty in the world and what can be done about it. Today, I'll outline the main _____ of the story, and then I'll tell you how I feel about it. At the end you'll have a chance to _____ your opinion.

Body

So, what did I find out? _____ to the article, the three richest people in the world have more wealth than the 48 poorest countries in the world. That's one quarter of all the world's countries! The article also said that one in two children lives in poverty – a shocking statistic. And it went _____ to say that 27,000 children die every day from extreme poverty – that's one child every three seconds!

The article also _____ at education. It said that one billion people entered the 21st century unable to read or sign their names. The article stated that 10 billion dollars would be enough to put every child into school. That's a lot of money, but did you know that it's less than one percent of what the world spends every year on arms?

Well, I'm glad to say that the news in the article wasn't all bad. It _____ on to _____ that there are many nongovernmental organizations and charities that are helping poor people, and that some businesses and corporations are also helping. For example, have you heard of Product Red? Did you know that if you buy a Product Red iPod, Apple gives a portion of the purchase price to the Global Fund, which helps fight disease in Africa? And it doesn't cost you anything extra!

Conclusion

I think this story is _____ and moving. It made me feel hopeful, however, when I read about the work of the _____ organizations. Maybe I can't do a lot myself, but if we all help a little, it'll _____ a big difference. Now I'd like to hear your views on this topic, especially your ideas about what we can do to help people who are living in poverty.

Presentation skills focus

1 Leading a group discussion

It's common to finish a presentation by leading the audience in a short discussion. This involves opening, continuing, and closing the discussion.

🔘 26   Are these sentences used to open, continue, or close the discussion? Write them in the correct section below. Then listen and check your guesses.

✓ • Now I'd like to hear your views.
  • Can anyone add to that?
  • I'd like to invite you to share your ideas.
  • We've heard a lot of great ideas today.
  • That's all the time we have. Thanks for sharing your views.

  • Now it's your turn to voice your opinions.
  • Do you all agree?
  • Thank you for participating today.
  • What do you think, Mark?

Open

• *Now I'd like to hear your views.*
•
•

Continue

•
•
•

Close

•
•
•

Presentation tip

• A discussion leader's job is to encourage audience participation. If someone is very quiet, you can say, "Emi, what do you think?" or "Emi, how about you?"
• When you ask a question, wait a few seconds for someone to answer. If no one does, call on someone.

2　Your turn

A Read the example from a discussion about a news-story presentation. Underline the sentences that are used to lead the group discussion.

Mari Now it's your turn to voice your opinions. Do you think we should try to help stop poverty, or should we leave it to the government and world leaders?

Jack I think it should be up to governments and leaders, especially the governments of poor countries. They should do more.

Mari Do you all agree?

Eva Well, I agree that governments should do more, but I think we should *all* try to help, too.

Mari Can anyone add to that?

Jack Yes, I think Eva is right. We should definitely try to help.

Mari Good point. Well, everyone, that's all the time we have. Thanks for sharing your views.

B Work in groups of three. Read the example in Exercise A aloud. Change roles twice.

C Complete the group discussion with sentences from page 76. (There is more than one correct answer.)

Classmate 1 _____
What do you think are the real keys to happiness?

Classmate 2 Well, in my opinion, having a job that you enjoy is the most important thing.

Classmate 1 _____

Classmate 3 I don't think that's true. I think spending time with family and friends makes us happier than spending time at work.

Classmate 1 _____

Classmate 2 Maybe, but I still think enjoying your work is important.

Classmate 1 Good point. _____

D Work with your group from Exercise B. Read the discussion in Exercise C aloud. Change roles twice.

Now **present yourself!**

- **Turn to page 78.**
- **Prepare your presentation.**

Present yourself! Give a presentation about a news story.

1 Brainstorming

Choose a current news story. Write it in the center of the brainstorming map.
Then read an article or listen to a TV or radio report about your news story.
Write as many details as you can for each brainstorming topic.

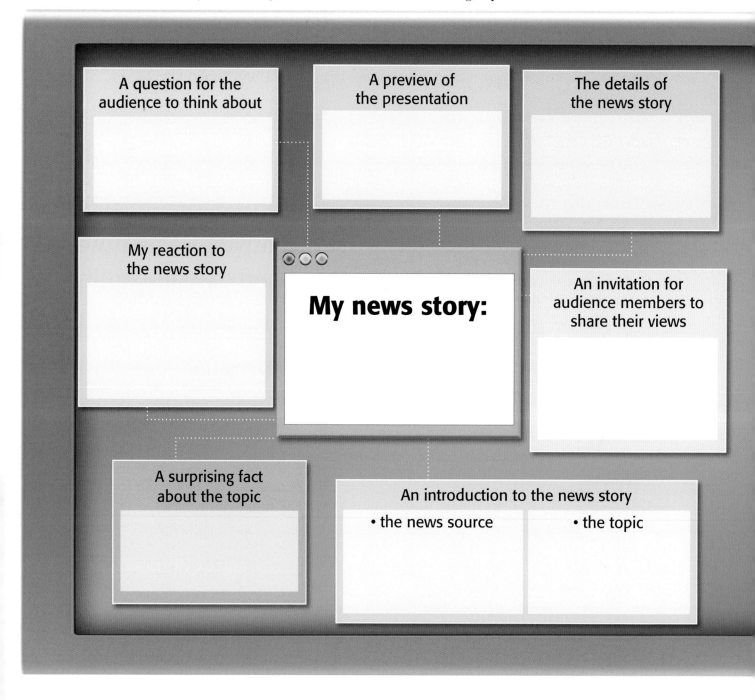

A question for the
audience to think about

A preview of
the presentation

The details of
the news story

My reaction to
the news story

○ ○ ○

My news story:

An invitation for
audience members to
share their views

A surprising fact
about the topic

An introduction to the news story

• the news source

• the topic

2) Organizing

Use your brainstorming notes from Exercise 1 to complete the outline.
Then make note cards from your outline and practice your presentation.

_____
(title)

I.   Introduction

    A. A question for the audience to think about

    _____

    B. A surprising fact about the topic

    _____

    C. An introduction to the news story
        • the news source: _____
        • the topic: _____
    D. A preview of the presentation

    _____

    _____

II. Body
    The details of the news story

    _____

    _____

    _____

    _____

III. Conclusion

    A. My reaction to the news story

    _____

    B. An invitation for audience members
        to share their views

    _____

3) Presenting

Give your presentation to the class.
Remember to lead a group discussion at the end.

Don't forget to complete
your self-evaluation on
page 85 after your presentation.

Unit 1 Self-evaluation

A motto for life

Read each statement. Circle, ☺, ☺, or ☹. Then write comments that will help you improve next time.

		Comments
I chose a motto that shows my personal values and was interesting to my audience.	☺ ☺ ☹	
I practiced enough before giving my presentation.	☺ ☺ ☹	
I explained the meaning of my motto and talked about a past experience related to it.	☺ ☺ ☹	
I followed the "dos and don'ts" for presentation notes from the *Presentation skills focus* lesson on page 16.	☺ ☺ ☹	
In my conclusion I clearly explained how the motto helps me in life.	☺ ☺ ☹	
My presentation was the right length.	☺ ☺ ☹	
I felt confident when giving my presentation.	☺ ☺ ☹	
I am satisfied with my presentation.	☺ ☺ ☹	

One thing that I did well was _____

_____

_____ .

One thing that I would like to do better for my next presentation is _____

_____

_____ .

Unit 2 Self-evaluation

Young people today

Read each statement. Circle, ☺, ☺, or ☹. Then write comments that will help you improve next time.

		Comments
I chose a survey topic that was interesting to my audience.	☺ ☺ ☹	
I practiced enough before giving my presentation.	☺ ☺ ☹	
I gave my audience enough information about my survey group.	☺ ☺ ☹	
I used visual aids and phrases for explaining visual aids from the *Presentation skills focus* lesson on pages 28 and 29.	☺ ☺ ☹	
In my conclusion I summarized my survey results.	☺ ☺ ☹	
My presentation was the right length.	☺ ☺ ☹	
I felt confident when giving my presentation.	☺ ☺ ☹	
I am satisfied with my presentation.	☺ ☺ ☹	

One thing that I did well was _____

_____

_____ .

One thing that I would like to do better for my next presentation is _____

_____

_____ .

Unit 3 Self-evaluation

Dream vacation

Read each statement. Circle, ☺, ☻, or ☹. Then write comments that will help you improve next time.

		Comments
I chose a vacation destination that was interesting to my audience.	☺ ☻ ☹	
I practiced enough before giving my presentation.	☺ ☻ ☹	
In my introduction I used lead-in questions from the *Presentation skills focus* lesson on page 40.	☺ ☻ ☹	
I gave my audience enough useful and interesting information about my topic.	☺ ☻ ☹	
In my conclusion I mentioned the cost of the vacation and length of stay.	☺ ☻ ☹	
My presentation was the right length.	☺ ☻ ☹	
I felt confident when giving my presentation.	☺ ☻ ☹	
I am satisfied with my presentation.	☺ ☻ ☹	

One thing that I did well was _____

_____

_____ .

One thing that I would like to do better for my next presentation is _____

_____

_____ .

How the world works

Read each statement. Circle, ☺, ☻, or ☹. Then write comments that will help
you improve next time.

		Comments
I chose a process that was interesting to my audience.	☺ ☻ ☹	
I practiced enough before giving my presentation.	☺ ☻ ☹	
In my introduction I used expressions for inviting audience questions from the *Presentation skills focus* lesson on page 52.	☺ ☻ ☹	
I used the words *first*, *second*, *next*, and *final* to explain the stages of the process.	☺ ☻ ☹	
In my conclusion I reviewed the stages of the process and recommended further reading.	☺ ☻ ☹	
My presentation was the right length.	☺ ☻ ☹	
I felt confident when giving my presentation.	☺ ☻ ☹	
I am satisfied with my presentation.	☺ ☻ ☹	

One thing that I did well was _____

_____ .

One thing that I would like to do better for my next presentation is _____

_____ .

Unit 5 Self-evaluation

In my opinion

Read each statement. Circle, ☺, ☺, or ☹. Then write comments that will help you improve next time.

		Comments
I chose an issue that was interesting to my audience.	☺ ☺ ☹	
I practiced enough before giving my presentation.	☺ ☺ ☹	
I gave strong supporting evidence for my opinion.	☺ ☺ ☹	
I used expressions to emphasize my opinion from the *Presentation skills focus* lesson on page 64.	☺ ☺ ☹	
In my conclusion I summarized my main points.	☺ ☺ ☹	
My presentation was the right length.	☺ ☺ ☹	
I felt confident when giving my presentation.	☺ ☺ ☹	
I am satisfied with my presentation.	☺ ☺ ☹	

One thing that I did well was _____
_____
_____ .

One thing that I would like to do better for my next presentation is _____
_____
_____ .

In the news

Read each statement. Circle, ☺, ☺, or ☹. Then write comments that will help you improve next time.

		Comments
I chose a news story that was interesting to my audience.	☺ ☺ ☹	
I practiced enough before giving my presentation.	☺ ☺ ☹	
In my introduction I gave the source, the main topic, and a preview of my presentation.	☺ ☺ ☹	
I gave my audience enough information about the details of my news story.	☺ ☺ ☹	
I used expressions for leading a group discussion from the *Presentation skills focus* lesson on page 76.	☺ ☺ ☹	
My presentation was the right length.	☺ ☺ ☹	
I felt confident when giving my presentation.	☺ ☺ ☹	
I am satisfied with my presentation.	☺ ☺ ☹	

One thing that I did well was _____

_____

_____ .

One thing that I would like to continue to work on in the future is _____

_____

_____ .

Acknowledgments

Illustration credits

Phil Hankinson: 12, 58
Jui Ishida: cover
R. Ricardo: 3, 16, 40, 52, 64, 76

Photography credits

2 ©Inmagine.
5 ©Inmagine.
8 *(clockwise from top left)* ©Inmagine; ©Inmagine; Taxi/Getty Images; ©Inmagine; ©Inmagine; Riser/Getty Images.
10 *(left to right)* ©Shioguchi/Getty Images; ©Shioguchi/Getty Images; ©Inmagine.
13 ©Shutterstock.
15 ©Shutterstock.
19 ©Dennis Kitchen Studio Inc.
20 *(top to bottom)* ©Shutterstock; ©Shutterstock; ©Inmagine.
22 *(clockwise from top left)* ©Inmagine; ©Inmagine; ©Inmagine; ©Inmagine.
24 ©Inmagine.
25 ©Shutterstock; ©Shutterstock.
27 ©Shutterstock.
31 ©Dennis Kitchen Studio Inc.
32 *(clockwise from top left)* ©Panthera Productions/Getty Images; ©Isu/Getty Images; ©Inmagine; ©Inmagine; ©Inmagine; ©Inmagine.
34 *(left to right)* ©Joseph Van Os/Getty; ©Inmagine; ©Inmagine.
36 ©Inmagine.
37 *(top to bottom)* ©Inmagine; Robert Francis/Photolibrary.
39 ©Shutterstock.
43 ©Dennis Kitchen Studio Inc.
46 *(left to right)* ©Ghislain & Marie David de Lossy/Getty; ©Inmagine.
48 ©Luis Veiga/Getty Images.
49 *(top to bottom)* ©Shutterstock; ©istockphoto.
51 ©Shutterstock.
55 ©Dennis Kitchen Studio Inc.
60 ©Shutterstock.
61 *(top to bottom)* ©Shutterstock; ©Inmagine.
63 ©Shutterstock.
67 ©Dennis Kitchen Studio Inc.
68 *(clockwise from top left)* ©Inmagine; ©Inmagine; Marco Simoni/Getty Images; ©John E Marriott/Alamy; ©Joe Drivas/Getty Images; ©Mike Goldwater/Alamy.
69 ©Shutterstock.
70 *(left to right)* ©Mitchell Funk/Getty Images; ©Inmagine; ©Inmagine.
71 ©Photolibrary RF/Photolibrary.
72 ©Barbier Bruno/Photolibrary.
73 ©Shutterstock.
75 ©Map Resources.
79 ©Dennis Kitchen Studio Inc.

Audio CD track listing

The audio CD contains the audio exercises for *Present Yourself 2, Viewpoints.*

Unit	Page	Exercise	Track
Getting ready	3	2B	2
Getting ready	5	2B	3
1	10	1A, 1B	4
1	11	2A, 2B	5
1	13, 14	2, 4	6
2	22	1A, 1B	7
2	23	2A, 2B	8
2	25, 26	2, 4	9
2	28	1B	10
3	34	1B	11
3	35	2A	12
3	37, 38	2, 4	13

Unit	Page	Exercise	Track
4	46	1A, 1B	14
4	47	2A	15
4	49, 50	2, 4	16
5	58	1B, 1C	17
5	59	2A	18
5	61, 62	2, 4	19
5	64	1A	20
5	64	1B	21
5	65	2A	22
6	70	1B	23
6	71	2A, 2B	24
6	73, 74	2, 4	25
6	76	1	26